VISIONARY WOMEN COLLECTIVE

INVESTABLE, TRANSACTABLE & COLLABORATABLE WOMEN OF INDIA

KADAMBARI UMAPATHY

ISBN
Hardcase 979-8-89277-253-2
Paperback 979-8-88975-583-8

Contents

WOMEN ENTREPRENEURSHIP DEVELOPMENT ORGANISATION

About WEDO

Empowering Women Entrepreneurs: Unleashing Potential with WEDO

In 2015, the Women Entrepreneurship Development Organisation (WEDO) embarked on a pioneering journey, dedicated to nurturing and advancing women entrepreneurs. With a profound commitment to fostering innovation, leadership, and growth among women, WEDO has emerged as a trailblazer in the realm of women's entrepreneurship.

Empowering Initiatives

WEDO stands as a beacon of support, offering an array of resources, mentorship programs, and networking opportunities tailored to the unique needs of women entrepreneurs. The organisation hosts an impressive suite of initiatives, each designed to provide women with the tools and guidance they need to thrive in their entrepreneurial ventures.

1. Women Entrepreneurs Collaborators Club

At the heart of WEDO lies the Women Entrepreneurs Collaborators Club. This groundbreaking platform serves as India's first collaborative and growth marketing community exclusively for women. Here, urban and semi-urban women entrepreneurs, adept at navigating the digital landscape, come together to expand their businesses. Through collaborations with like-minded entrepreneurs from diverse corners of India, members of this club are empowered to explore new horizons in business.

2. Visionary Women Circle

The Visionary Women Circle, an exclusive community within WEDO, brings together accomplished women from diverse industries. This dynamic network enables women to forge meaningful relationships, expand their reach, and strengthen their personal brand. Within this circle, women gain access to potential investors, strategic partners, and influential mentors, providing them with the support needed to accelerate business growth.

3. Visionary Women Awards

Recognizing excellence is at the core of WEDO's mission. The Visionary Women Awards celebrate the achievements and contributions of exceptional women entrepreneurs. Through this platform, WEDO aims to highlight their expertise, accomplishments, and entrepreneurial spirit, inspiring others and creating a community of visionary women.

4. Visionary Women Conference

The Visionary Women Conference serves as a dynamic platform for women entrepreneurs to come together, share knowledge, and foster collaborations. This event provides an opportunity for women to engage in meaningful discussions, gain insights from industry leaders, and explore new avenues for growth and development.

Collaborative Ecosystem

WEDO understands that success in entrepreneurship requires a supportive ecosystem. To this end, the organisation collaborates with funding agencies, incubators, and other stakeholders. This collaborative approach ensures that women entrepreneurs have access to a comprehensive array of resources, making WEDO a one-stop solution for all their entrepreneurial needs.

Through its visionary initiatives and collaborative approach, WEDO is not only shaping the landscape of women-led businesses but also empowering a new generation of women entrepreneurs to reach unprecedented heights of success. With a steadfast commitment to inclusivity and empowerment, WEDO continues to be a driving force in advancing women in the business world.

Write to: <u>kadambari@wedo.org.in</u>

About
Visionary Women Project

The Visionary Women Project

Introducing "The Visionary Women Project," curated by WEDO - Women Entrepreneurship Development Organisation, dedicated to propelling and empowering women

entrepreneurs. In India, while there is a wealth of women entrepreneurs and professionals, identifying them remains a challenge. The The Visionary Women Project seeks to provide a platform for showcasing the incredible talents of Indian women. This initiative comprises three distinctive components focused on recognition, personal branding, visibility, and fostering a community of visionaries poised to accelerate together. The primary goal is to identify accomplished women, give them the recognition they deserve, amplify their presence, and assist them in propelling their businesses. Read on to explore the unique features of this transformative project.

The Visionary Women Circle

The Visionary Women Circle is an exclusive community designed for visionary businesswomen poised to elevate their enterprises.

We firmly believe in the collective strength of women collaborating to expand their networks and spheres of influence. As members, women will connect with accomplished peers across diverse industries, fostering meaningful relationships and broadening their spheres of impact. We offer a structured framework to bolster their personal brand and amplify their influence. This circle provides access to a network of potential investors, strategic partners, and influential mentors, all dedicated to accelerating business growth. Cross-learning opportunities and knowledge-sharing sessions will further fuel their journey to success. Being a part of the Visionary Women Circle means surrounding oneself with exceptional individuals, leveraging powerful connections, and redefining the essence of a visionary woman in the world of business.

The Visionary Women Collective

The Visionary Women Collective is an extraordinary compendium featuring the professional and business narratives of extraordinary women. This unique collection serves as a magnet for potential collaborators, investors, partners, and opportunities for the featured visionary women. Within these pages, readers will discover a mosaic of profiles highlighting the expertise, achievements, and entrepreneurial zeal of these exceptional women. Each biography offers a glimpse into their professional odysseys, illuminating their triumphs, experiences, and the invaluable contributions they have made in their respective domains. The Visionary Women Collective transcends a mere anthology of biographies; it stands as a formidable platform that links aspiring collaborators, investors, partners, and individuals seeking fresh opportunities with these visionary women. By presenting their profiles, we invite readers to explore potential synergies, establish meaningful connections, and nurture mutually beneficial partnerships. These women embody the essence of entrepreneurship, showcasing resilience, innovation, and an unwavering pursuit of excellence. Their stories reflect a diverse array of industries, experiences, and accomplishments, underscoring the immense talent and potential embedded within women-led ventures. I encourage you to immerse yourself in the realm of the Visionary Women Collective and unearth the treasure trove of talent, expertise, and transformative ideas that these women bring to the forefront. As you delve into their professional and business chronicles, envision the possibilities that arise from engaging with these visionary women and the dynamic collaborations that can flourish. Together, let us celebrate and champion the remarkable achievements of these visionary women and harness the force of collaboration to propel innovation, growth, and triumph. With eager anticipation, Kadambari Umapathy Entrepreneur & Curator Visionary Women Collective.

About She Finance

She Finance: Empowering Women to Build Legacies Through Funding Excellence!

She Finance is an initiative by WEDO. At She Finance, we recognise the unparalleled potential that women-owned businesses bring to the entrepreneurial landscape. We are committed to  fueling your journey, not just with funds, but with the support and resources necessary to build a lasting legacy. If you are a woman with a vision, She Finance is here to be your financial partner on the path to success.

Funding Your Dreams, Building Your Legacy

She Finance understands that financial support is a crucial catalyst for turning dreams into reality. Our funding programs are tailored to address the specific needs of women entrepreneurs, providing not only capital but a strategic partnership for sustainable growth.

Key Features of She Finance Funding

- *Tailored Financing Solutions:* We understand that every business is unique. Our funding solutions are customised to meet your specific requirements, ensuring that you receive the support you need to thrive.

- *Transparent Processes:* She Finance values transparency. Our application and approval processes are clear and straightforward, allowing you to focus on what you do best – building and growing your business.

- *Mentorship Alongside Funding:* Beyond financial support, She Finance offers mentorship programs to guide you through the challenges of entrepreneurship. Benefit from the experience and wisdom of successful mentors who have walked a similar path.

- *Networking Opportunities:* As a She Finance beneficiary, you become part of a dynamic community of women entrepreneurs. Leverage this network to forge valuable connections, collaborate, and share experiences with like-minded individuals.

Your Legacy Awaits - Apply for She Finance Funding Today! **Write to:** support@wedo.org.in

If you are a woman-owned business with a vision for building a legacy, She Finance invites you to explore our funding opportunities. Transform your aspirations into achievements with the financial backing and strategic support that She Finance provides.

From the Desk of
Dr. Abdul Manaff

Chairman, First Holdings International, WEDO, VWC

"The Visionary Women Collective," a project that aims to celebrate the remarkable achievements of women who have gone above and beyond, leaving an indelible mark on society, is definitely a wonderful initiative and I would like to place on record my unconditional support to all the endeavours.

As WEDO embarks on this endeavour, I wanted to share some words of encouragement and wisdom to inspire both the women profiled in this collective and those who read their stories. In the pursuit of excellence and personal growth, it's essential to remember the words of Gary Ryan Blair: "Do more than is required. What is the distance between someone who achieves their goals consistently and those who spend their lives and careers merely following? The extra mile." These words encapsulate the spirit of the collective and the women who are featured. Throughout history, visionary women have shattered barriers, defied expectations, and paved the way for future generations. They didn't settle for the status quo; instead, they pushed themselves to go beyond what was expected of them. Their determination to travel the extra mile opened doors to new opportunities and led to remarkable achievements.

Kadambari Umapathy and her visionary organisation, WEDO (Women Entrepreneurship Development Organisation), exemplify the essence of women who dare to be different and go the extra mile to create a brighter future. Her journey, along with the collective effort of WEDO, serves as an inspiring tale of resilience, determination, and a commitment to opening doors to new opportunities and personal growth.

Kadambari, a trailblazing leader and a driving force behind WEDO, has consistently demonstrated her belief in breaking free from conventions and paving unique paths. Her story is a testament to the transformative power of dedication and innovation. WEDO, under Kadambari's guidance, has been a beacon of hope for women from all walks of life.

This visionary organisation has faced numerous challenges, ranging from societal norms to institutional barriers, yet it has persevered and thrived. The women of WEDO have shown that it's not enough to meet the status quo; they have actively sought to exceed expectations and broaden horizons. Through their unwavering dedication, Kadambari and WEDO have not only created opportunities for themselves but have also extended their hand to lift others up. They understand that success is not a solitary journey; it's a collective effort that involves empowering one another.

In a world where women often face hurdles, Kadambari and WEDO serve as an inspiration to those who aspire to create change. They remind us that by thinking differently, working tirelessly, and pushing boundaries, we can transcend limitations and reach new heights. Their story is a shining example of the belief that every woman has the potential to be a visionary, a trailblazer, and a catalyst for positive change.

As we compile the stories of these extraordinary women, let us remember the following quotes as we encourage others to take the path less travelled:

1. "Life shrinks or expands in proportion to one's courage." – Anais Nin

2. "The question isn't who is going to let me, it's who is going to stop me." – Ayn Rand

3. "I never dreamed about success. I worked for it." – Estée Lauder

4. "You are the one that possesses the keys to your being. You carry the passport to your own happiness." – Diane von Furstenberg

These words are a testament to the power of determination and the willingness to do more than what's required. They remind us that success is not handed to us; it's earned through consistent effort and a commitment to going that extra mile. So, whether you find yourself in your career or personal life, always remember that the extra mile can lead to remarkable achievements and a more fulfilling journey.

As we celebrate their achievements and their unwavering commitment to personal growth and empowerment, let us be inspired to follow in their footsteps, to challenge the status quo, and to keep doors open to new opportunities for women everywhere. Let us celebrate the women who have blazed this trail and inspire others to follow in their footsteps.

With warm regards and a shared vision for a brighter future,

Dr. Abdul Manaff
Chairman, First Holdings International
WEDO, VWC

Kadambari Umapathy

About Kadambari Umapathy

Founder, WEDO (Women Entrepreneurship Development Organisation)

Kadambari Umapathy is a visionary entrepreneur and the Founder of WEDO (Women Entrepreneurship Development Organisation). With a passion for empowering women in the business world, Kadambari has dedicated herself to creating opportunities and resources for aspiring women entrepreneurs.

Under her dynamic leadership, WEDO has become a trailblazer in the field of women's entrepreneurship. Kadambari's innovative approach led to the establishment of India's first collaborative and growth marketing community exclusively for women. This platform has revolutionised how urban and semi-urban women entrepreneurs expand their businesses in the digital age.

Kadambari's commitment to fostering an inclusive ecosystem for women entrepreneurs is evident in WEDO's initiatives, including the Visionary Women Circle, Visionary Women Awards, and Visionary Women Conference. These programs provide women with the tools, mentorship, and networking opportunities needed to thrive in their entrepreneurial ventures.

With a deep understanding of the challenges and opportunities facing women in business, Kadambari collaborates with funding agencies, incubators, and stakeholders to offer comprehensive solutions for entrepreneurial needs. Her leadership and vision continue to inspire and drive the progress of women-led businesses, making a significant impact on the entrepreneurial landscape.

"I'm Safe" App: Empowering Women Safety Through Technology

The "I'm Safe" revolution in today's India, the crying need for women's safety has found a huge ally with technology. Pioneered by Chennai-based founders, Samson Selladurai and Giftson Selladurai, "I'm Safe" isn't merely an app—it's a groundbreaking initiative aimed at combating rape, domestic violence, and all forms of abuse against women. Leveraging advanced features like location tracking, blockchain, and cryptography, the vision behind "I'm Safe" is to ensure the safety of one billion women worldwide. The I'm Safe Personal Women Safety App is a FREE tool tailored exclusively for women. Its "track me" feature allows real-time location sharing, offering peace of mind to both users and their loved ones. In case of an emergency, a discreet SOS alert can be activated, promptly notifying designated contacts. Furthermore, a "Fake Call" function helps women tactfully exit unsettling situations, while the Anonymous Recording feature can assist during internal inquiries. Essential helplines come pre-loaded, ensuring timely help is always at one's fingertips. Organisations and universities aren't left out either. I'm Safe Org offers an integrated platform for POSH Grievance Redressal, enabling employees and students to voice concerns, even anonymously. Emergency SOS alerts connect users with pertinent personnel, ensuring timely intervention. With features like "Org Help" and a dedicated admin dashboard, institutions can holistically address safety and information concerns. With a goal as noble as eradicating abuse against women, "I'm Safe" is more than just technology; it's hope, empowerment, and a beacon of security in uncertain times. It's a testament to how innovation can reshape societal challenges and pave the way for a safer India for women. With more than 10,000 downloads & translations in Hindi and Tamil, it's available for FREE on both the Android and the App store. More details on the FREE app can be found at www.imsafe.app

The Visionary Women Circle stands behind the "I am Safe" initiative and extends heartfelt support to Samson Selladurai and Giftson Selladurai for all their commendable efforts!

"Naturals Salon": Empowering Women Through Entrepreneurship and Redefining Beauty Standards

"Naturals Salon": Pioneering a movement towards a Housewife-free India, empowering women through entrepreneurship and redefining beauty standards.

Naturals Salon is on a mission to liberate Indian women from traditional roles, aiming to create a society where women are financially independent and empowered. Founded by K. Veena and later joined by co-founder and CEO C.K. Kumaravel, Naturals Salon has revolutionised the beauty industry in India.

Since its inception in the early 2000s, Naturals Salon has rapidly expanded to become India's foremost chain of hair and beauty salons, with over 650 outlets nationwide. The vision for 2025 is even more ambitious: a goal of 3000 salons, alongside the empowerment of 2000 women entrepreneurs and the creation of 1,00,000 jobs.

Central to Naturals Salon's ethos is the belief in the potential of women as thriving entrepreneurs. By providing robust support and resources, they have facilitated the rise of 400 women business owners in just over two decades. This initiative not only transforms lives but also reshapes societal norms, demonstrating that women can lead, innovate, and excel in the business world.

Naturals Salon is not just a beauty establishment; it's a movement for change. Their mission to build a 'housewife-free India' is a testament to their dedication to women's economic empowerment and their belief in the power of entrepreneurship. In every salon, in every venture, Naturals Salon is leaving an indelible mark on the path to a more inclusive, equal, and self-sufficient India.

VISIONARY WOMEN ENTREPRENEURS

Dhivya Sriram

About Dhivya Sriram's Venture: Anil Engineering Pvt. Ltd.

Anil Engineering Pvt. Ltd. (AEPL), stands as a distinguished name in the engineering landscape, with a legacy of excellence that spans over half a century. This ISO 9001:2015 certified company has cemented its reputation as a trailblazer, offering world-class products under the banner of "Made in India." AEPL's commitment to pioneering innovation and sustainability places it at the forefront of technological advancement in the ever-evolving gas storage industry. With a dedicated research and development team, they tirelessly explore cutting-edge technologies and incorporate environmentally friendly materials and practices into their operations, demonstrating their dedication to a greener future. AEPL's hallmark is tailored excellence, offering personalised support and services to clients, with a team of over 50 technical experts crafting custom solutions. Their

AEPL: Shaping the Future of Gas Storage Technology

dedication to quality shines in the domain of LPG safety fittings, where they have delivered over 10,000 innovative products, including LPG storage tanks and patented LPG vaporisers, solidifying their position as a reliable partner in the gas storage industry. As AEPL sets its sights on entering the Saudi Arabia market, pursuing an IPO pathway, and increasing export turnover by 12%, its trajectory promises growth and global impact.

Anil Engineering Pvt. Ltd. (AEPL), has a diverse array of potential customer segments owing to its versatile gas storage solutions. First and foremost, the oil and gas industry represents a significant clientele, where AEPL - The technocrat organisation offers products required for the storage and handling of liquefied petroleum gas (LPG), anhydrous ammonia and other liquefiable gases like EO, VCM, N2. Anil Engineering also supports complete turnkey projects for LPG or LNG and offers excellent service pan-India and globally.

Their products are designed and manufactured to meet the most stringent quality standards, adhering to customer-specific requirements and international guidelines.

Their commitment to excellence has earned them the trust of over 800+ clients, including PSU oil companies and prestigious Indian and international organisations like BPCL, IOCL, HPCL, SHV Energy, Elf Gas, Hindustan Zinc Ltd., L&T, Godrej, Tata Motors, Tata Steels, AMW, Ford Motors, etc.

About Dhivya Sriram

Dhivya Sriram, a process optimization work expert working towards continuous improvement and the Director of Anil Engineering Pvt. Ltd. (AEPL), Director at VS Pressure Vessels and Gas Projects, and Proptirix of ALG Equipments Asia Pacific, is a visionary leader reshaping the engineering landscape. With a people-oriented approach, she fosters a workplace culture valuing her dedicated workforce. Armed with an MA in Human Resource Management, she skillfully navigates HR complexities, ensuring a motivated and committed team. Dhivya's expansion initiatives, market studies, product scope analysis, and niche market development, have propelled AEPL into international markets, turning it into a global brand. As a determined go-getter, she aims for a 40%+ market share in international geographies, and as a woman leader, she uplifts lives through her journey and ethical values. Dhivya champions sustainability, promoting green futures with her companies and innovative ideas for a brighter tomorrow, all while embodying resilience and the mantra: "it's ok to fall; remember to pick yourself up, shake yourself, and go on again."

Prospects for Dhivya Sriram: Anil Engineering Pvt. Ltd.

The path ahead is illuminated with plans, strategies, and initiatives that beckon AEPL. Currently, an extensive market research study is underway in Saudi Arabia, aimed at unveiling potential buyers and expanding export reach. This pursuit resonates with a commitment to exploring new horizons and broadening global presence.

Five years into the future, a strategic spark ignites—an IPO. This aspiration holds transformative potential, with the groundwork set to materialise over the next two to three years.

Anil Engineering Pvt. Ltd. (AEPL), has a diverse array of potential customer segments owing to its versatile gas storage solutions. First and foremost, the oil and gas industry represents a significant clientele, where AEPL can cater to the storage needs of oil refineries, gas processing plants, and distribution networks. Additionally, the food processing industry can benefit from AEPL's solutions, particularly in the safe storage of gases used in food production. The construction and infrastructure sector forms another valuable segment, where AEPL's products can be instrumental in welding, heating, and powering various equipment. Furthermore, manufacturers seeking specialised gas storage solutions for their production processes and government entities focusing on gas safety regulations can also find value in AEPL's offerings. Lastly, as AEPL expands into international markets like Saudi Arabia, it can target clients within these segments, aiming to serve diverse industries and contribute to their safe and efficient gas storage needs.

Collaborators for Anil Engineering Pvt. Ltd.

- Research institutions, technology providers, and environmental organisations make good collaborators who can join in co-creating cutting-edge solutions.

Clients for Anil Engineering Pvt. Ltd.

- Companies operating in the oil and gas industry seek precise and secure gas storage solutions within the oil and gas sector.

- Industries involved in food processing seek efficient gas handling solutions for their operations within the food processing industry.

- Manufacturers with specialized gas storage needs seek companies offering tailored solutions that align with their specific production processes.

- Government entities focusing on gas safety extend their influence through agencies and organizations that prioritize gas safety regulations and standards.

- Industries with bottling plants require precise gas storage and handling due to the nature of their operations.

- Companies involved in the production of pressure vessels ensure safe gas storage.

- Entities involved in turnkey projects related to LPG or LNG can rely on AEPL for comprehensive support in gas storage solutions.

Potential Investors for Anil Engineering Pvt. Ltd.

- AEPL presents an exciting investment opportunity with plans for global expansion, including entry into new markets like Saudi Arabia.

- An IPO pathway and ambitious export goals are part of AEPL's growth strategy.

Write to: dhivya@aeplglobe.com

Manju S M

About Manju S M's Venture: Finestra

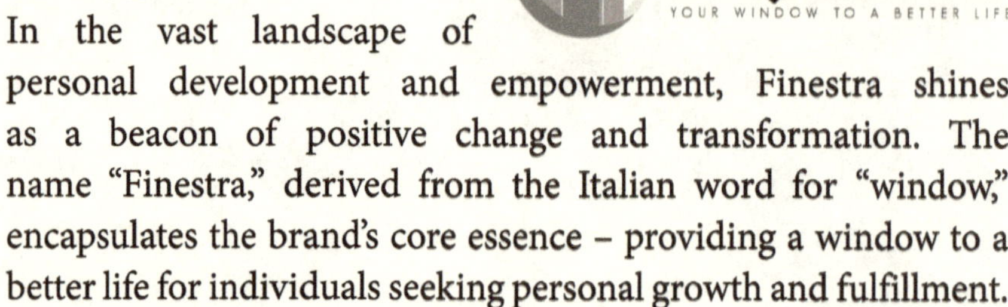

In the vast landscape of personal development and empowerment, Finestra shines as a beacon of positive change and transformation. The name "Finestra," derived from the Italian word for "window," encapsulates the brand's core essence – providing a window to a better life for individuals seeking personal growth and fulfillment.

At Finestra, the mission is clear: to empower lives through comprehensive life coaching services. The brand offers a diverse range of coaching services, with a particular focus on parenting coaching. It is dedicated to guiding parents on a journey towards a more blissful and fulfilling parenting experience.

The tagline, "Your Window To a Better Life," reflects the profound commitment of Finestra to open doors of opportunity and self-discovery for its clients. Each coaching session serves as a window through which individuals can explore their potential, set meaningful goals, and navigate the path to personal growth.

> **Finestra:** Your Window to a Better Life

Finestra's parenting coaching services stand as a testament to its holistic approach to life empowerment. Parenthood is a journey filled with challenges and joys, and Finestra is there to provide the guidance and support needed to navigate this intricate path. Through expert coaching, parents can unlock the secrets to more joyful, balanced, and effective parenting.

With a commitment to transformation and a dedication to providing individuals with the tools and insights needed to lead better lives, Finestra exemplifies the power of coaching in driving positive change. It is not merely a brand but a trusted partner on the journey towards personal growth and fulfillment. As one peers through the window that is Finestra, they will find a world of possibilities and the keys to unlocking their true potential.

About Manju S M

Manju S M is a remarkable individual whose journey from engineering to life coaching has been marked by a profound commitment to personal development and empowerment. Armed with a diverse array of certifications and expertise, she stands as a beacon of positive change in the lives of those she serves.

With a background in engineering, Manju embarked on a transformative path to become a certified Purpose Coach. Her dedication to helping individuals discover their true calling and passion shines through in her work. Additionally, she is a certified Emotional Intelligence Practitioner, emphasizing the importance of emotional well-being in personal growth.

What sets Manju apart is her extensive knowledge of neuroscience for personal development, neuroscience for parenting, mindful parenting, and mindfulness-based cognitive therapy. These certifications underscore her deep understanding of the intricate workings of the human mind and the profound impact they can have on personal growth and relationships.

Manju's contributions to the field of personal development extend to the realm of literature. She is a published author, with her book titled "Decode Your Dream Career." In this work, she offers valuable insights and guidance to individuals seeking clarity and direction in their career paths.

Through her multifaceted expertise and unwavering dedication, Manju S M has transformed herself into a beacon of hope and empowerment for those on a journey of self-discovery and personal growth. Her journey from engineering to life coaching is a testament to the power of passion and purpose in leading a fulfilling life. As a certified Purpose Coach, Emotional Intelligence Practitioner, and author, Manju continues to inspire and guide individuals towards their dreams and aspirations.

Prospects for Manju S M: Finestra

Collaborators for Finestra

- Collaborating with parenting, child development, and family dynamics workshop organisers, Finestra aims to expand its service offerings through parenting workshops and seminars.

- Collaborating with licensed child psychologists and counselors who specialize in child behavior, development, and mental health ensures a holistic parenting approach.

- Collaborating with parenting book authors or recognized experts in parenting and child development provides Finestra's clients with valuable insights and resources.

- Collaborating with pediatricians, nurses, and healthcare professionals facilitates the sharing of resources and information to support parents.

- Daycare centers, preschools, and early education providers with expertise in child development can provide additional resources and support for parents seeking childcare and early education centres.

- Licensed family therapists and counselors who specialize in family dynamics, communication, and relationships, offering holistic support to families through collaboration.

- Collaborating with online parenting communities and forums dedicated to discussions and support could expand Finestra's reach and provide a platform for sharing valuable information.

- Educational consultants and tutors specialise in education and academic support for children, offering resources and guidance on educational strategies through collaboration.

- Therapists, counselors, and wellness experts who offer services related to mental health and well-being are great partners for collaboration for Finestra, providing additional resources for parents dealing with stress and mental health challenges.

- Parenting bloggers and influencers find collaboration opportunities with Finestra, where they can share expertise on parenting, family life, and child development through guest posts, webinars, or joint events with a wider audience.

Clients for Finestra

- Parents seeking guidance can find expert coaching and support to navigate the challenges and joys of parenthood.

- Individuals seeking personal growth, those on a journey of self-discovery and personal development, are looking for guidance and tools to lead more fulfilling lives.

- Individuals striving for better life balance, seeking to achieve a better balance in various aspects of their lives, including work, family, and personal well-being.

- Couples seeking coaching to enhance their parenting skills and strengthen their partnership in raising children, aimed at strengthening their parenting dynamic.

- Individuals facing specific parenting challenges, such as communication issues with their children, behavioral concerns, or managing work-life balance, can find expert coaching and support.

- Parents of children with special needs, requiring specialized coaching and support in navigating the unique challenges associated with raising children with special needs.

- Providing expert coaching and support tailored for individuals going through significant life transitions, such as becoming new parents, transitioning to a new phase of life, or facing career changes.

- Professionals seeking work-life balance solutions are working individuals looking for strategies to balance career aspirations with their roles as parents and individuals.

- Parents striving for more effective communication seek coaching to improve their communication skills with their children and foster positive relationships within the family.

- Individuals seeking personal fulfillment find tools, insights, and support to lead more fulfilling and purpose-driven lives.

Write to: smmanju@gmail.com

Dimple Gaikwad

About Dimple Gaikwad's Venture:
Pearl International & Pearl Immigration

Since its establishment in 2011, Pearl International & Pearl Immigration have been at the forefront of facilitating seamless international transitions for individuals seeking new horizons. The company operates as a licensed entity, specializing in aiding clients in obtaining citizenship and residency through strategic investments across 20+ countries. With a rich history spanning over a decade, Pearl's migration experts have garnered the trust of investors for their unparalleled expertise in citizenship-by-investment programs. Their proficiency extends to the intricate realm of real estate investments associated with these programs, as well as a comprehensive understanding of the tax implications involved.

In parallel to their migration services, Pearl International excels in global recruitment. They connect clients with highly skilled candidates from mid to senior levels across a diverse spectrum of sectors. Backed by a strong presence in 130 offices worldwide, Pearl International provides advanced recruitment consultancy and talent acquisition services. Their brand, technology, and professional business model afford them the strength to offer tailor-made solutions.

> **Pearl International & Pearl Immigration:** Pioneering Global Ventures in Citizenship and Residency

Pearl International's consultants specialise in Information Technology, Accounting & Finance, Operations, and Sales & Marketing, delivering a comprehensive range of recruitment solutions. Whether it's traditional hiring or project-related endeavours, they ensure a seamless process. Over the years, they've continuously refined their internal processes, training, and methodologies to align with client needs and market dynamics.

The driving force behind Pearl International's entrepreneurial journey lies in their understanding of the critical role adaptation plays in thriving in new environments. They recognise that embracing change, particularly in a new culture or language, is a continuous process, demanding a re-evaluation of familiar norms and a commitment to personal growth.

Looking ahead, Pearl International envisions a future focused on global readiness, cross-border integration, and enhanced investment in mobility and immigration expertise. Their goal is to further enhance their capacity to serve individuals seeking new opportunities on a global scale.

What sets Pearl International apart is their truly international scale combined with unparalleled local knowledge and expertise. With physical offices in 35 countries, operated by local recruitment experts with decades of industry experience, Pearl International ensures that their consultants understand the local culture, language, and market dynamics. This ensures that they can offer personalised assistance to job seekers regardless of the country they are exploring.

Pearl International's commitment to its clients is reflected in their meticulous and highly professional hiring procedures. They offer continuous support throughout the hiring process and beyond, helping candidates stand out in a crowded job market. Their collaborations with a diverse array of global clients provide candidates with exceptional career opportunities.

In summary, Pearl International & Pearl Immigration stand as beacons of excellence in facilitating international transitions and providing top-tier recruitment consultancy. With their unwavering commitment to client satisfaction, they continue to be a driving force in the realm of global ventures.

About Dimple Gaikwad

Dimple Gaikwad, the visionary founder of this dynamic venture, possesses a unique perspective on the future of migration, education, and career development. Her entrepreneurial journey began with a profound understanding of the challenges individuals face when transitioning to a new country. Recognizing that adaptation is not a one-time event, but a continuous daily requirement, Dimple set out to address this critical need.

Coming from a background where privilege and wealth did not exempt her from the demands of adaptation, Dimple understood the transformative power of change. She realised that to thrive in a new culture, one must be willing to reexamine the familiar and make significant shifts in thinking and behavior.

Dimple's venture, grounded in the belief that immigrants bring invaluable contributions to entrepreneurship and employment growth, has established itself as a leader in facilitating seamless transitions for individuals seeking new opportunities abroad. With a strong commitment to a growth mindset, Dimple's company, Pearl Immigration, empowers clients to recognise the boundless potential within themselves. By fostering a culture of hard work, innovative strategies, and open collaboration, Dimple ensures that her clients achieve remarkable outcomes, surpassing the limitations of fixed mindsets.

In terms of revenue streams, Dimple's company has positioned itself as a global player in the international migration and recruitment space. Officially recorded remittance flows are projected to exceed impressive figures, underlining the substantial impact of Dimple's ventures on the global landscape.

Looking ahead, Dimple envisions an even more inclusive and globally-oriented future. Her aspirations encompass a multifaceted approach, including initiatives like global readiness, integration of cross-border experiences into business operations, and investment in mobility and immigration expertise. Dimple is committed to prioritizing international and cross-cultural experiences in recruitment strategies, recognizing the rich diversity of perspectives that immigrants bring to the workplace. She places significant value on multilingualism and adaptive mindsets, seeking candidates who embody these qualities. Additionally, Dimple encourages her employees to seek international experiences, fostering a culture of continuous learning and growth within her organisation.

Dimple's dreams extend beyond personal success to the broader vision of creating a more interconnected and culturally diverse world. Her innovative approach to business, driven by a profound understanding of the challenges immigrants face, sets her apart as a visionary leader in the field of international migration and recruitment.

As Dimple continues to lead the way in global ventures, she extends an open invitation to prospective clients, collaborators, and investors who share her vision for unlocking new horizons and embracing the potential of a rapidly changing world. Together, they aim to build bridges that transcend borders, creating a future of limitless opportunities for individuals and businesses alike.

Prospects for Dimple Gaikwad: Pearl International & Pearl Immigration

Collaborators for Pearl International & Pearl Immigration

- Collaborating with language training centres to offer comprehensive language programs for clients.

- Partnerships with educational consultants to provide end-to-end services for students seeking admission abroad.

- Collaborating with legal experts who specialize in immigration law ensures compliance and facilitates smooth immigration processes.

- Joint efforts with career advisors ensure holistic services for professionals seeking international opportunities in collaboration with career counselors.

- Collaborating with tech companies to leverage technological advancements in the immigration process, technology firms actively seek ways to enhance efficiency and innovation.

Clients for Pearl International & Pearl Immigration

- Aspiring students exploring new educational opportunities, seeking admission to universities in their favorite countries.

- Professionals pursuing career growth find opportunities by advancing their careers through migration to countries with promising job markets and growth prospects.

- Individuals with entrepreneurial aspirations looking to establish or expand their businesses in foreign markets.

- Language learners, interested in acquiring new languages as part of their adaptation process to new cultures and environments.

- High net-worth individuals (HNIs) seek investment or business expansion opportunities abroad, reflecting their significant financial resources.

- Corporate entities requiring assistance in navigating immigration and mobility solutions for their international workforce.

- Universities and educational institutions seeking partners to assist their students in the immigration process.

- Language schools and institutes facilitate smoother transitions for immigrants by offering language training programs.

Potential Investors for Pearl International & Pearl Immigration

- Investors interested in supporting innovative startups in the field of immigration and education services.

- Private equity investors seek opportunities with established companies exhibiting a proven track record of success, similar to Pearl Immigration.

- High net-worth individuals seeking to invest in promising ventures with a social impact, such as facilitating global education and migration, are often referred to as angel investors.

- Impact investors, focusing on ventures that create positive social and environmental impact and aligning with Pearl Immigration's mission, contribute to the company's growth and purpose.

- Corporate investors, companies seeking diversification in their portfolio, focus on investing in promising startups within the immigration and education sector.

Write to: info@pearlimmigration.org

TIME
FOR
SALES

MVP
14
days
Minimum Viable
Product

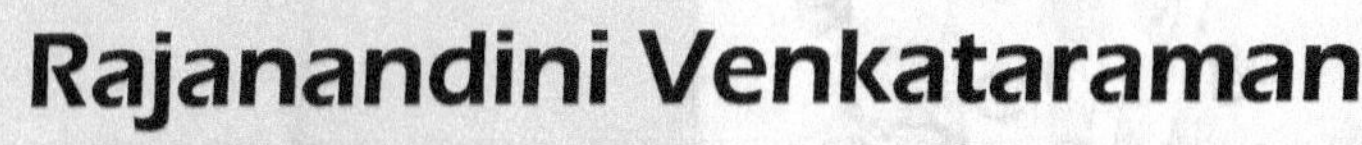

Rajanandini Venkataraman

About Rajanandini Venkataraman's Venture - Swomb Technologies

Swomb Technologies, co-founded by Rajanandini Venkataraman in September 2022, stands as a visionary tech partner for startups with ambitious dreams. Their distinctiveness lies in their remarkable ability to deliver a Minimum Viable Product (MVP) within a mere 14 days and an enterprise-scale product in 45 days offering unparalleled support to startups striving to realise their grand visions in today's fast-paced and disruptive market landscape. Their cutting-edge digital product, "TYMEBOT", revolutionises the concept of time, overcoming the challenges posed by time constraints and empowering startups to thrive in the dynamic business environment.

Swomb Technologies: Empowering Businesses with Transformative Technology Solutions and Driving Digital Revolution with Expertise and Innovation

Swomb Technologies goes beyond startups, extending their expertise to mainstream businesses with their comprehensive enterprise support systems. They are dedicated to providing "Tech solutions to real problems for businesses." With a diverse clientele spanning industries such as logistics, waste management, fintech, and hospital management systems, Swomb Technologies brings innovative and tailored technological solutions to address the specific challenges faced by businesses across various sectors.

About Rajanandini Venkataraman

Rajanandini Venkataraman is a seasoned professional with a diverse range of experience across various roles snd industries.

Currently serving as the Chief Executive Officer at Swomb Technologies and Services Pvt. Ltd., she has been leading the company since September 2022. Prior to her role at SWOMB Technologies, she worked as the Chief Marketing Officer at D. Fame Tech Pvt. Ltd. for 4 years and 2 months. She also held positions as a Business Development Manager and Senior Business Development Executive at different organisations. With her background in recruitment consulting and HR consulting, she brings a well-rounded perspective to her leadership role. Rajanandini's experience showcases her proficiency in business development, marketing, and HR management.

Prospects For Rajanandini Venkataraman: Swomb Technologies

Collaborators for Swomb Technologies

- Tech startups in need of reliable partners to develop and launch innovative concepts.

- Enterprises seeking tailored tech solutions to enhance their operations and productivity.

- Business channel partners interested in collaborating with Swomb Technologies for customer acquisition.

- Tech talents with exceptional skills and expertise in the digital domain.

Clients for Swomb Technologies

- Startups with scalable tech ideas in need of development and implementation.

- Enterprises looking for effective tech solutions to address operational challenges and improve efficiency.

- Businesses seeking specialised tech services to enhance productivity in various verticals.

Potential Investors for Swomb Technologies

- Private equity firms focusing on the tech sector.

- Investors keen on supporting emerging tech ventures.

- Technology investment groups looking for promising startups.

- High net-worth individuals with an interest in cutting-edge technology ventures.

Write to: nandy@swomb.app

Adhilakshmi Logamurthy

About Advocate Adhilakshmi Logamurthy

Advocate Adhilakshmi Logamurthy is an eminent legal practitioner with a distinguished career. She is also an accredited mediator with the High Court - Madras and the Singapore International Mediation Institute (SIMI); she brings a wealth of expertise and unwavering dedication and passion to her profession.

At the core of her work lies a profound commitment to address critical issues affecting vulnerable segments of society including, women, children, transgender persons, senior citizens, differently abled individuals and those who need legal support. Advocate Adhilakshmi Logamurthy is a tireless advocate for positive societal change, employing a multifaceted approach encompassing litigation, mediation, and training, all with the overarching goal of fostering a fairer and more equitable world.

Her legal acumen spans a diverse spectrum of vital domains, including social beneficial legislations (pertaining to women, children, transgender persons, senior citizens, differently abled and labour), matrimonial issues, domestic violence, workplace harassment, property rights and drafting (including commercial contracts), with a deeply rooted commitment. Advocate Adhilakshmi Logamurthy serves as a guiding light for those in need, providing invaluable legal support while relentlessly working to shape a society that is more equitable.

> **Advocate Adhilakshmi Logamurthy:** Championing for Legal Rights Being the Voice of the Voiceless with Unwavering Dedication

Throughout her illustrious career, Advocate Adhilakshmi Logamurthy has garnered numerous awards and accolades, recognizing her exceptional contributions to the legal field and her tireless advocacy for marginalised communities. Her dedication for creating a more equitable and society has not only earned her professional acclaim but has also positively impacted countless lives.

Furthermore, her active contribution to print and electronic media, in particular, her television and YouTube shows, has provided a platform to amplify her advocacy efforts and promote legal awareness among the general public. Through these shows, Advocate Adhilakshmi Logamurthy has effectively disseminated her legal expertise and insights, furthering her mission of creating a more informed and equitable society.

Advocate Adhilakshmi Logamurthy is trained in NLP. Law being her profession, training and coaching are her passion, many of her clients have benefited from her motivational sessions. She is also a most wanted motivational speaker.

Prospects for Advocate Adhilakshmi Logamurthy

Collaborators for Advocate Adhilakshmi Logamurthy

- Small, medium-scale industries, individuals, corporates, educational institutions and enterprises in need of Prevention of Sexual Harassment (POSH) (Internal Committee Member) and POCSO (Protection of Children from Sexual Offences) training. Advocate Adhilakshmi Logamurthy is actively seeking partnerships and collaborations.

- Advocate Adhilakshmi Logamurthy is open to collaborating with corporates and individuals to contribute to the evolving legal landscape through mediation services.

- Advocate Adhilakshmi Logamurthy is open towards soft skill training and life coaching and willing to collaborate with like-minded individuals or organisers.

Clients for Advocate Adhilakshmi Logamurthy

- Individuals in need of legal assistance in matters related to social beneficial legislations (pertaining to labour, women, children, transgender persons, senior citizens, differently abled), matrimonial issues, domestic violence, workplace harassment, property rights and drafting including commercial contracts, or other legal issues, can benefit from Advocate Adhilakshmi Logamurthy's expertise and consultation and mediation services.

- Aspiring lawyers and junior legal practitioners seeking guidance and mentorship can collaborate with Advocate Adhilakshmi Logamurthy to enhance their legal knowledge and skills.

Potential Investors for Advocate Adhilakshmi Logamurthy

While Advocate Adhilakshmi Logamurthy's focus is primarily on providing legal assistance and training. She is also seeking investors who share her vision and are interested in supporting initiatives related to the prevention of domestic violence, sexual harassment, elderly abuse and other legal issues. This includes providing legal support for individuals and corporates. Investors may find opportunities to invest in projects aligned with her mission.

Write to: advocateadhilogu@gmail.com
           advadhilogu93@gmail.com

YOUR POTENTIAL IS
ENDLESS
Aruna V N

About Aruna V N's Venture: Yoga-Darshini

Yoga-Darshini

Yoga-Darshini, a transformative initiative, was born from the profound vision of Param Pujya Guruji Swami Tejomayananda of Chinmaya Mission. Its very name, carefully chosen by Guruji Himself, reflects its profound purpose - to see and reveal the glorious essence of Yoga. This remarkable endeavour stands as an embodiment of love and gratitude towards the revered Masters, offering an opportunity to serve humanity through the life-changing teachings of Yoga.

At its core, Yoga-Darshini is a beacon of holistic well-being, catering to diverse needs through a range of offerings that span the realms of online and offline instruction, as well as corporate well-being programs. Through its online platforms, it reaches seekers far and wide, providing access to the timeless wisdom of Yoga. The offline experience, guided by dedicated instructors, brings the authentic essence of Yoga to life, fostering a deeper connection between mind, body, and soul. Furthermore, Yoga-Darshini extends its benevolent influence into corporate spaces, promoting well-being and balance amidst the demands of the modern workplace.

Yoga-Darshini: Illuminating the Path of Yoga

Yoga-Darshini aims to make yoga accessible - not only in terms of the practices but also in terms of finance and time. Yoga-Darshinis way of teaching ensures that the immense benefits of yoga can be reaped even by the busiest individuals by easily incorporating it in their everyday lives without demanding too much of their time.

In essence, Yoga-Darshini is not merely an institution; it is a sacred journey, a tribute to the wisdom of the Masters, and a profound service to humanity, offering the gift of Yoga as a transformative force for a healthier, more balanced, and spiritually enriched life.

"Youga," an online product offered by Yoga-Darshini, presents an enticing opportunity for potential investors. This innovative online platform leverages the profound wisdom of Yoga and Vedanta to promote physical and mental well-being, making it an appealing investment prospect for those keen on the holistic wellness industry. With its commitment to delivering transformative experiences and its potential for scalability in the digital space, "Youga" is poised to attract investors who seek to support the growth of wellness-focused online ventures.

About Aruna V N

Aruna VN, a native of Chennai, stands as a testament to the harmonious fusion of an accomplished academic and corporate background with a profound dedication to the realms of yoga and Vedanta philosophy. Armed with degrees in Electronics and Communication Engineering and Business Administration, she embarked on a successful career within the sphere of top-tier international commercial banks.

However, the call to delve deeper into the profound teachings of yoga and Vedanta eventually became irresistible. In December 2016, Aruna obtained her training certification from the revered Sivananda Yoga Vedanta Centre in Madurai, setting the course for her transformational journey as a yoga instructor. Since that pivotal moment, she has committed herself to disseminating the profound wisdom and benefits of yoga to others through her teaching.

Aruna's unwavering commitment to her own personal growth is exemplified by her continuous pursuit of knowledge and mastery in the field. In February 2020, she completed an intensive Sadhana course, further enhancing her expertise and understanding of yoga.

What distinguishes Aruna is her unique blend of experience as a triathlete and marathon runner. This athletic background provides her with a distinctive advantage in crafting yoga sessions and classes designed not only to promote physical well-being but also to nurture mental strength and resilience.

Aruna VN's journey as a yoga instructor has been characterised by inclusivity and a far-reaching impact. Her teaching has touched diverse groups, ranging from corporate environments to educational institutions, individuals with special needs and their caregivers, avid runners seeking balance and endurance, yoga studios, and individuals seeking holistic health and well-being.

Beyond the physical and mental dimensions of yoga, Aruna is an ardent student of Vedanta. She perceives yoga as a potent path for the evolution of the self, transcending mere physical fitness to facilitate inner growth and self-realization.

Aruna VN's profound reverence for these ancient practices, coupled with her unwavering dedication to sharing their transformative potential, positions her as a guiding beacon in the domain of yoga and holistic wellness.

Aruna is the Founder and Chief Trainer at Yoga-Darshini, a wellness organisation that focuses on teaching yoga and promoting holistic well-being.

She is internationally certified as a yoga trainer from the Sivananda Yoga Vedanta Centre in Madurai. Aruna has been practicing and teaching yoga since 2016, and she believes in going beyond just the physical postures (asanas) of yoga.

She aims to bring the ancient practices of yoga into every aspect of life, allowing individuals to incorporate them beyond the yoga mat.

Under Aruna's guidance, Yoga-Darshini has built a dedicated team of certified yoga teachers and wellness experts who have collectively accumulated over 5000 hours of teaching experience.

Prospects for Aruna V N: Yoga-Darshini

Collaborators for Yoga-Darshini

- Yoga-Darshini is open to collaborating with experienced yoga instructors for offerings on the platform, providing users with a well-rounded yoga experience. In return, instructors gain access to a wider audience and the credibility of being associated with Yoga-Darshini.

- Partnering with professionals in holistic health can provide users with a comprehensive approach to well-being. These practitioners can offer specialised knowledge in areas such as nutrition, mindfulness, and alternative therapies, while benefiting from increased exposure and potential client referrals.

- Influencers in the fitness and wellness space can help increase brand visibility and reach a wider audience interested in holistic well-being. They can promote Yoga-Darshini's offerings to their followers and potentially engage in joint marketing efforts.

- Offering nutrition advice and meal plans as part of the well-being journey can be a valuable addition. Nutritionists benefit by reaching a new audience and potentially gaining clients interested in improving their dietary habits.

- Collaborating with retreat centres can provide opportunities for users to attend in-person workshops, intensives, or retreats, enhancing the offline experience. Retreat centres benefit from increased visibility and potentially attract new participants to their events.

- Collaborating with educational institutions can offer specialised programs for students, teachers, and staff to incorporate well-being practices into their routines. Educational institutions benefit from access to a structured well-being program that complements their existing offerings.

- Partnering with companies interested in offering wellness programs to their employees. Companies benefit from providing their employees with access to a comprehensive well-being platform, potentially leading to a healthier and more productive workforce.

Clients for Yoga-Darshini

- Individuals seeking holistic well-being find comprehensive support, as they look to improve their overall well-being through yoga and holistic wellness practices.

- Individuals working in corporate environments who are interested in incorporating yoga and wellness into their daily routines for stress relief and better work-life balance.

- People with specific needs or conditions that can benefit from adaptive yoga practices, as well as their caregivers seeking to support their well-being, encompass individuals with special needs and their caregivers.

- Avid runners and athletes seeking to enhance their physical performance, flexibility, and mental resilience through yoga.

- Existing yoga studios and wellness centres can enhance their offerings by incorporating Aruna's expertise and teachings in the realm of yoga and wellness.

- Schools or educational institutions interested in providing yoga and wellness programs for students, faculty, and staff.

- Individuals who are passionate about maintaining a healthy and balanced lifestyle and are seeking guidance from a qualified yoga instructor.

- Individuals interested in Vedanta philosophy explore the spiritual and philosophical aspects of yoga as taught by Aruna, who seamlessly integrates Vedanta philosophy into her teachings.

- Management training and research organisations like MANTRA show interest in incorporating yoga and wellness training as part of their programs.

- Triathletes and Marathon runners find value in yoga to enhance their endurance sports training, aiming to improve flexibility, recovery, and mental focus.

- Individuals interested in understanding and practicing the deeper aspects of yoga beyond physical postures seek to incorporate yoga beyond asanas.

- Wellness enthusiasts interested in online platforms may explore holistic well-being through platforms like "Youga," a potential offering by Yoga-Darshini.

Potential Investors for Yoga-Darshini

- Individuals passionate about holistic well-being, yoga, and Vedanta as avenues for personal growth and spiritual development.

- Impact investors interested in supporting ventures that promote mental and spiritual health.

- Angel investors seeking opportunities in the wellness and personal development sector.

- Investment firms with a focus on holistic health and wellness initiatives.

- Yoga enthusiasts and practitioners looking to invest in businesses aligned with their interests and values.

Write to: arunavn@yahoo.in

Subangi Umapathy

About Subangi Umapathy's Venture: Tulips & Daffodils

Tulips & Daffodils is a sanctuary for plant enthusiasts and nature lovers alike.

Here, the essence of nature is harnessed to offer a range of nutrition-rich and chemical-free products designed to enhance the well-being of plants and soil. The vital connection between healthy plants and a thriving ecosystem is deeply understood, fueling the mission to provide premium, environmentally friendly plant and soil care solutions.

At Tulips & Daffodils, sustainability is at the core of their ethos. The belief is firmly held that the key to vibrant and resilient plants lies in utilizing nature's own nutrients and elements. A dedicated team of horticulturists, practicing agriculture experts, and agriculture students collaborate to create innovative products that are both plant friendly and ecologically responsible

Tulips & Daffodils: Cultivating Natural Growth

The product portfolio features a diverse array of nutrition-rich natural formulations, meticulously crafted to cater to the unique needs of various plant species and growth stages. From chemical-free fertilizers and soil conditioners to natural pest repellents and growth stimulants, each of Tulips & Daffodils product is made with the finest and responsibly-sourced ingredients.

The commitment to chemical-free solutions extends beyond plant health, ensuring the well-being of families, pets, and the environment, as harmful synthetic chemicals and toxins are avoided. Whether an individual is an experienced gardener or just beginning their green journey, Tulips & Daffodils stands as a trusted partner in nurturing lush and thriving plant life.

The customer-centric approach means that expert advice and support are readily available to ensure the most fruitful gardening endeavours. Join in cultivating a greener future and experience the magic of nature's goodness with Tulips & Daffodils, where plants flourish naturally.

Tulips & Daffodils is committed to making gardening an essential life-skill for the next generation. To achieve this goal, the brand has developed tailor-made kits designed specifically for children. These kits serve a dual purpose: they engage kids in enjoyable learning experiences while instilling important morals and life skills.

Through their custom kits for children, the brand sparks creativity and teaches responsibility to children. Their products are carefully curated to instil vital life-skills like self-confidence, empathy, time-management etc., while the children relish growing their plants. Their chemical-free products are being used by several schools and families making gardening a safe-play for the kids and stress-free for their parents and the schools as they teach the children valuable information about the food source.

Tulips & Daffodils range of environment-conscious plant-based gifts like potted-plants, garden kits and other botanical delights stand as testament towards the brand's commitment towards sustainability in all walks of life and greener earth.

About Subangi Umapathy

Subangi Umapathy, the driving force behind Tulips & Daffodils, is a true visionary who's deeply passionate about nature and committed to sustainable gardening. Her deep affection for greenery and her desire for future generations to enjoy chemical-free food have sparked her vision of a world where nature flourishes in perfect harmony.

With her dedication to plant well-being and a strong focus on environmental preservation, Subangi leads a team of experts. Together, they carefully create premium products designed to nurture natural growth while staying true to sustainability principles.

Guided by her unwavering commitment to a greener tomorrow, Subangi's journey unfolds as plants flourish and the beauty of nature takes centre stage. Her impressive academic background, including an MBA and MCA degree, along with 15 years of corporate experience in senior HR roles, provides a solid foundation for her mission to promote sustainable gardening practices.

Prospects for Subangi Umapathy: Tulips & Daffodils

Collaborators for Tulips & Daffodils

- Partnering with research institutions can drive innovative product development. Research collaborations can help in creating cutting-edge, science-backed solutions for plant and soil care.

- Collaboration with environmental NGOs promotes sustainable practices and can help in spreading awareness about the importance of eco-friendly gardening.

- Collaborations with agricultural universities can facilitate research and development, ensuring that the products are tailored to meet the specific needs of various plant species.

- Partnering with local nurseries expands product distribution and allows Subangi's products to reach a broader customer base, including both home gardeners and commercial gardeners.

- Collaborating with other eco-conscious brands can lead to co-branded initiatives that further promote sustainability and eco-friendly practices.

  Interior architects can collaborate with Subangi and enhance the value they provide by incorporating green interior elements into their clients' envisioned dream spaces.

  Event organisers can team up with Subangi to include sustainable and eco-friendly plant-based gifting options as part of event planning.

Clients for Tulips & Daffodils

- Enthusiasts passionate about sustainable gardening, looking for chemical-free and environmentally friendly plant-care solutions, find valuable resources in the offerings tailored for home gardeners.

- Schools and colleges interested in eco-friendly programs can be potential clients. These institutions can incorporate Subangi's products into their gardening and landscaping efforts.

- Businesses involved in horticulture and landscaping can benefit from Subangi's natural plant and soil care solutions to maintain healthy landscapes, specifically targeting commercial gardeners.

- Environmental enthusiasts will find Subangi's products aligning with their values, as they are individuals dedicated to eco-friendly practices and environmental preservation.

- Businesses engaged in greenhouse cultivation can use Subangi's products to ensure the health and vitality of their greenhouse plants, addressing the needs of plant growth and development.

Corporate clients can provide their employees with chemical-free green interior spaces, courtesy of Tulips & Daffodils' green interior services.

Potential Investors for Tulips & Daffodils

- Impact investors who support ventures promoting sustainability and environmentally responsible practices may be interested in investing in Tulips & Daffodils.

- Investors specializing in agriculture and horticulture may see the potential for growth in Subangi's eco-friendly plant and soil care solutions.

- Dedicated environmental funds focused on supporting eco-conscious businesses can be a source of investment.

- Angel investors who seek promising startups with a sustainability focus can provide valuable funding for the project.

Write to: Tulipsanddaffodils2019@gmail.com

Vvarsharani Agare

About Vvarsharani Agare's Venture: Digital Techists Consulting

Digital Techists Consulting, an upcoming and highly recommended digital marketing services provider in Pune, is at the forefront of empowering businesses with a strong online presence. With their expert professional team, they offer a comprehensive range of solutions to meet the evolving needs of their clients.

Their services encompass a wide spectrum of digital marketing strategies, including Search Engine Optimization (SEO), Social Media Optimization (SMO), targeted advertising campaigns, and much more. As industry experts, they stay abreast of the latest trends and technologies, ensuring that their clients receive cutting-edge solutions to stay competitive in the digital landscape.

Digital Techists Consulting: Pioneering Digital Metamorphosis and Crafting Strategies to Propel Businesses into a Realm of Sustainable Growth and Unrivaled Success

With a firm belief in customer satisfaction, Digital Techists Consulting strives to provide transparent business deals and build long-lasting relationships with their clients. They understand that a strong digital presence is essential for businesses to thrive in today's digital era.

Their branding strategy-based services are designed to cater to businesses, particularly those led by women entrepreneurs, whether they are product-based or service-based. By harnessing the power of digital marketing, Digital Techists Consulting enables businesses to reach a wider audience, engage with their target market, and achieve remarkable growth.

About Vvarsharani Agare

Vvarsharani Agare, a woman of extraordinary resilience and unwavering determination, has overcome immense challenges to forge a remarkable path of her own. Diagnosed with cancer at a young age, she experienced a profound shift in perspective, recognizing the inherent beauty and fragility of life. Hailing from a modest background in a small village, Vvarsharani's journey has been characterised by a relentless pursuit of knowledge and personal growth. Despite undergoing chemotherapy, she remained steadfast in her studies and successfully obtained a Bachelor of Science degree. Settling in Pune, she found herself inspired to make a mark in the world, driven by an innate desire to deviate from the conventional career path. With a resolute spirit and boundless curiosity, Vvarsharani embarks on a transformative journey of self-discovery, fueled by a burning passion to make a meaningful impact and chart her own course.

Prospects for Vvarsharani Agare: Digital Techists Consulting

Collaborators for Digital Techists Consulting

- Technology consulting firms.

- Software development companies.

- IT service providers.

- Web development agencies.

- Digital marketing agencies.

Clients for Digital Techists Consulting

- Businesses in need of digital transformation solutions.

- Startups looking to establish a strong online presence.

- Companies seeking to optimise their digital marketing strategies.

- Organisations aiming to streamline their operations through technology.

- E-commerce platforms looking for technology-driven solutions to enhance user experience.

Potential Investors for Digital Techists Consulting

- Private equity firms specializing in the tech sector.

- Angel investors focused on supporting emerging tech ventures.

- Technology investment groups.

- High net-worth individuals with a keen interest in digital technology startups.

Write to: admin@digitaltechists.in

Rekha Suresh

About Rekha Suresh's Venture: V2 Advocates

V2 Advocates stands as a comprehensive solution for all business legal compliance needs, offering a unique advantage over engaging with multiple legal consultants or firms. Advocate M.P. Rekha Suresh, an internationally renowned Trademark Attorney and Start-Up Advisor, leads this venture with a diverse legal background.

Advocate Rekha's profile encompasses a broad spectrum of legal roles, including corporate advocacy, intellectual property law, authorship of the acclaimed book "Brand Sutra," academia, research, training, and mentoring for start-ups. Her passion extends beyond advocacy, encompassing education, skill development, and legal compliance guidance for emerging businesses.

> **V2 Advocates:** Pioneers in IP & Corporate Law; Transforming Legal Landscapes

Established in 2016, V2 Advocates swiftly became a leader in providing Intellectual Property services in India and beyond. The firm excels in Intellectual Property Rights, Litigations, Property Due Diligence, Documentations, and Corporate Disputes. Their commitment to excellence has garnered awards and accolades, solidifying their position in the legal domain.

The firm operates with a collaborative approach, working closely with IP lawyers to safeguard clients' interests across all business levels. V2 Advocates specialises in offering strategic advice, management, and implementation of IP protection strategies, ensuring clients derive maximum benefit from their intellectual property assets.

V2 Advocates' vision is to be the forefront service provider for International Intellectual Property Protection. Their mission extends beyond legal services, aiming to educate clients on the pivotal role of Intellectual Property in the modern market-driven economy.

Areas of Expertise/UVP

- Trademark

- Copyright

- Design

- Patent

- Geographical indication

- Corporate business

- Property documentation

- Title verification

- Litigation

- Incorporation

Notable Credentials

- Panel advocate and legal advisor for numerous corporates, pharmaceutical manufacturing companies, and NRIs.

- Mentor in AIC-Anna University Incubation Foundation.

- Successfully filed and registered over 700 trademarks.

- Guided numerous start-ups in brand and invention protection as a mentor.

- Winner of the Glass Ceiling Award for Best Law Firm in 2022.

- Winner of Latchya Magudam Awards 2022 and Philanthropic Icon Award for 2022.

About Advocate Rekha Suresh

Advocate Rekha Suresh is an eminent figure in the legal domain, renowned for her extensive knowledge and expertise in various facets of law. With a distinguished career spanning corporate advocacy, intellectual property law, academia, and mentoring, she has left an indelible mark on the legal landscape.

As an International Trademark Attorney and Start-Up Advisor, Advocate Rekha possesses a wealth of experience and a keen insight into the intricacies of legal compliance. Her multifaceted role extends beyond the confines of a courtroom; it encompasses the realms of authorship, research, and training. She is the proud author of the highly acclaimed book "Brand Sutra," a testament to her depth of understanding in the field.

Advocate Rekha's passion for the law transcends the traditional boundaries of legal practice. She is equally dedicated to education, taking an active role in shaping the next generation of legal professionals. Her mentoring of start-ups in navigating the complex terrain of legal compliance is a testament to her commitment to fostering entrepreneurship.

In 2016, Advocate Rekha took a bold step by founding her own law firm, V2 Advocates. Under her astute leadership, the firm swiftly ascended to become a preeminent service provider for all Intellectual Property-related services in India and abroad. Their specialization in Intellectual Property Rights, Litigations,

Property Due Diligence, Documentations, and Corporate Disputes has earned them a reputation for excellence.

V2 Advocates distinguishes itself not only through its legal prowess but also through its unwavering dedication to professionalism, ethics, accountability, and efficiency. The firm's collaborative approach, working closely with IP lawyers, ensures that clients' intellectual property interests are safeguarded at every stage of their business endeavours.

Advocate Rekha's vision for V2 Advocates is nothing short of ambitious. She envisions the firm as the foremost service provider for International Intellectual Property Protection. Beyond legal services, she endeavours to educate clients on the pivotal role that Intellectual Property plays in the contemporary market-driven economy.

Advocate Rekha Suresh's accolades and recognitions are a testament to her exceptional contributions to the legal field. As a panel advocate and legal advisor for numerous corporates, pharmaceutical manufacturing companies, and NRIs, she has earned the trust and respect of her peers and clients alike.

Her role as a mentor at the AIC-Anna University Incubation Foundation underscores her commitment to nurturing young talent in the legal sphere. Having successfully filed and registered over 700 trademarks, she has demonstrated a remarkable track record in protecting intellectual property.

Advocate Rekha's achievements have been acknowledged with prestigious awards, including the Glass Ceiling Award for Best Law Firm in 2022, Latchya Magudam Awards 2022, and the Philanthropic Icon Award for 2022.

Prospects for Rekha Suresh: V2 Advocates

Collaborators for V2 Advocates

- Lawyers interested in international practice, particularly those with expertise in international law, especially in the context of intellectual property, could collaborate effectively with Advocate Rekha Suresh.

- Collaborating with financial experts can be invaluable, especially in matters related to intellectual property valuations, financial compliance, and taxation.

- Experts in corporate governance and compliance, company secretaries can play a crucial role in ensuring that businesses are legally sound.

- Marketing and branding professionals can work closely with Advocate Rekha to align legal strategies with branding efforts, ensuring brand protection and integrity.

- In today's digital age, collaborating with digital marketers can help in safeguarding intellectual property online and managing online reputations.

- Incubation cells, where organizations often nurture startups and entrepreneurs, provide opportunities for collaborating with them, offering early-stage legal guidance and compliance.

- Individuals and organisations involved in innovation can benefit from Advocate Rekha's expertise in protecting their intellectual property.

- Businesses involved in manufacturing may require specialised legal advice, particularly regarding intellectual property rights, product liability, and compliance.

- Providing legal advice and services to non-resident Indians often requires a unique set of skills and understanding of international law.

- Advocate Rekha's expertise in intellectual property law can be particularly valuable in the pharmaceutical industry, where patent protection is critical.

- Collaborating with legal advisors for corporations can lead to mutually beneficial partnerships in handling complex legal matters.

- Collaborating with educators and institutions allows for the exchange of knowledge and can lead to mentoring opportunities for students.

- Networking and collaborating with other professionals in the intellectual property field can lead to a wider range of services and expertise for clients.

Clients for V2 Advocates

- Businesses looking to expand internationally may include companies seeking to operate in multiple countries and requiring legal advice on international business practices.

- Individuals or groups embarking on new business ventures, particularly in areas like intellectual property, compliance, and business structure, need legal guidance, addressing the needs of entrepreneurs and start-ups.

- Companies involved in the production of goods may require legal assistance in areas such as contracts, patents, trademarks, and product liability.

- Individuals or organisations with innovative products or technologies that require protection through patents, trademarks, or other intellectual property rights.

- Larger organisations may need legal services for a variety of purposes, including compliance, litigation, contracts, and intellectual property matters.

- Companies operating in the pharmaceutical industry may require specialised legal advice, especially in relation to patents and regulatory compliance.

- NRIs may need legal assistance with matters related to their businesses or investments in India, or with international legal issues.

- Educational institutions may seek legal advice on matters related to intellectual property, compliance, or general legal education. Additionally, students may require mentoring or guidance in their legal careers.

Potential Investors for V2 Advocates

- Other law firms or legal professionals looking to expand their reach or services may see value in investing in a well-regarded firm like V2 Advocates.

- Investors specializing in technology, patents, or intellectual property may find V2 Advocates an attractive opportunity.

- Given the evolving landscape of legal technology, investors focused on legal tech startups or firms leveraging technology in their services might find V2 Advocates appealing.

Write to: legal@v2advocates.com

Dr. Siyarah

About Dr. Siyarah's Venture: "Fab Looks"

Dr. Siyarah is a multi-talented individual with a diverse range of achievements and contributions. As the fashion designer and owner of Fab Looks in New Delhi, she has created a brand that exudes style, creativity,

and elegance. With a comprehensive approach that encompasses stitching, designing, customising, and ready-mades since 2012, Fab Looks has become a go-to destination for fashion enthusiasts seeking all-in-one solutions. Furthermore, the recent launch of her brand "SIYARAH" on October 29, 2023, marks a significant milestone in her entrepreneurial journey. The brand, now open for franchising, invites aspiring entrepreneurs to join this exciting venture and be a part of Dr. Siyarah's transformative legacy.

Her entrepreneurial prowess has been recognised as she was awarded the prestigious title of Eminent Entrepreneur of the Year 2022 by the Dreamlife Foundation. This accolade speaks to her exceptional skills in managing a successful fashion business and providing top-notch services to her customers.

> **Fab Looks:** Unleashing Fashion Excellence since 2012—From Customised Creations to Ready-Made Perfection.

About Dr. Siyarah

Dr. Siyarah is a multifaceted individual whose influence transcends conventional boundaries. Not only is she a thriving entrepreneur, but her role as a motivational speaker sets her apart, inspiring countless individuals to chase their aspirations. Her ability to connect with audiences leaves an indelible mark, igniting a passion for self-realization and personal growth. Beyond the spotlight, Dr. Siyarah is a prominent figure in the world of fashion and entertainment, gracing runways and captivating audiences with her magnetic presence. Yet, her impact reaches far beyond glamour and fame. Dr. Siyarah's philanthropic endeavours are a testament to her compassion, as she actively advocates for the welfare of voiceless animals. This dedication to social work has earned her the esteemed Acharya Devo Bhava Award, a testament to her status as a distinguished philanthropist. Dr. Siyarah's list of accolades is nothing short of remarkable, including the Bharat Bhushan Award for her contributions to peace and human rights. She is celebrated as the Inspiring Woman Achiever of the Year 2022, a title that underscores her immense influence. Additionally, she holds the titles of Iron Lady of the Year 2023 and Inspiring Fashion Designer 2023, bestowed upon her by prestigious organisations. Dr. Siyarah's commitment to global peace is exemplified by her role as a Peace Ambassador, representing India on International Peace Day.

Prospects for Dr. Siyarah: Fab Looks

Collaborators for Fab Looks

- Fashion designers and stylists.

- Fabric suppliers and manufacturers.

- Marketing and branding agencies.

- Fashion photographers and videographers.

Clients for Fab Looks

- Individual fashion enthusiasts seeking personalised garments.

- Boutiques and fashion retailers.

- Event planners and stylists.

- Fashion influencers and bloggers.

- Celebrities and public figures.

Potential Investors for Fab Looks

- Fashion investment firms.

- Angel investors with a focus on emerging fashion brands.

- Private equity firms with a portfolio in fashion and retail.

- High net-worth individuals with an affinity for fashion startups.

Write to: team.siyarah@gmail.com

Shalini Chetan Kumar

About Shalini Chetan Kumar's Venture: f2f Designer Boutique

Introducing "f2f Designer Boutique" - where fashion dreams come to life at an affordable cost. With a steadfast commitment to customization and on-time delivery, this boutique has earned a reputation for excellence and unparalleled customer service.

At the heart of f2f Designer Boutique's offerings lies its specialty in crafting exquisite wedding outfits. From resplendent wedding gowns that exude grace and opulence to meticulously embellished aari work adorning wedding blouses, each creation is a testament to the artistry and craftsmanship that defines this establishment.

f2f Designer Boutique: Where Affordable Elegance Meets Bespoke Fashion Dreams

Beyond its focus on weddings, f2f Designer Boutique caters to the discerning fashion enthusiasts seeking personalised attire. Here, the creative team takes pride in translating individual visions into tangible sartorial marvels that reflect the unique essence of each client.

Not stopping there, the boutique extends its prowess to the realm of family fashion. f2f Designer Boutique offers thoughtfully curated family combos, designed with meticulous attention to detail, to create harmonious ensembles that celebrate unity and elegance.

The boutique's devotion to providing fashion for all extends to the little ones as well. Adorable and charming, the kids' wear collection enchants with its delightful designs, catering to the youngest fashion aficionados.

Recognizing the diverse needs of its clientele, f2f Designer Boutique has introduced rental services, a move that has garnered significant interest and expanded its customer base. This innovative offering allows individuals to revel in elegance for special occasions without compromising on financial prudence.

The boutique has discovered a world of fashion that's graced by celebrities and even Bigg Boss contestants. Their meticulously designed outfits have adorned some of the brightest stars, ensuring customers to shine like a celebrity in their exclusive creations.

In the fashion narrative scripted by f2f Designer Boutique, clients are not merely patrons; they are the protagonists of their style stories. The boutique's commitment to delivering quality, affordability, and custom excellence weaves an enthralling chapter in the fabric of timeless elegance, where fashion dreams find fulfillment in every stitch.

About Shalini Chetan Kumar

Shalini's Chetan Kumar's remarkable journey unfolds as she blends engineering expertise and an MBA with an unyielding passion for design. As a former logistics manager, her yearning for creativity led her to venture into the world of fashion. Through hard work, Shalini's boutique gained recognition by captivating fashion enthusiasts with unique and stylish clothing. Her engineering background streamlined operations, ensuring efficiency and quality, while her MBA knowledge fostered strong customer relationships. Today, Shalini stands as a triumphant entrepreneur, bridging engineering, business, and fashion, pursuing her true passion with dedication and fervour. Her narrative speaks of resilience, aspiration, and the fulfilment of a cherished dream—a testament to the power of following one's heart.

Prospects for Shalini Chetan Kumar: f2f Designer Boutique

Collaborators for f2f Designer Boutique

- Fabric manufacturers seeking exclusive collaborations to infuse designs with premium fabrics.

- Fabric sellers partnering to enrich the diversity of materials for readymade outfits.

- Readymade outfit dealers/sellers collaborating to expand visibility and choices for buyers.

- Export units facilitating seamless global reach through simplified shipping and logistics.

- Fashion designers converging creative visions for enriched designs and a broader appeal.

- Online retail platforms transforming into digital showrooms for global exposure.

- Fashion influencers amplifying brand resonance through effective digital engagement.

- International fashion events navigating global horizons for heightened brand visibility.

Clients for f2f Designer Boutique

- Individuals seeking unique and premium quality readymade outfits.

- Fabric retailers and sellers looking for diverse material options.

- Fashion enthusiasts in search of exclusive designs and curated collections.

Potential Investors for f2f Design Boutique

- Investors with an interest in the fashion and design industry.

- Private equity firms focusing on emerging fashion startups.

- High net-worth individuals with an affinity for the fashion and design industry.

Write to: f2fdesignerboutique@gmail.com

Rashmi Mandal

About Rashmi Mandal's Venture: RnT Designs

In the realm of contemporary architectural and interior design, a formidable force emerges - RnT Designs. Established in 2020 and headquartered in the bustling city of Faridabad, India, this modern firm boasts a diverse and unparalleled expertise, spanning a myriad of disciplines including commercial, residential, hospitality, mixed-use, and high-rise buildings, in addition to their meticulous focus on interior design.

At the core of RnT Designs lies an unwavering commitment to crafting evocative and immersive experiences through architecture, while astutely attending to the practical needs of clients, sites, and locales. Their unique approach and design strategies adeptly traverse the realms of intricate details to cohesive and holistic visions, seeking to explore the boundless potential of spaces and orchestrating an unparalleled experiential richness.

RnT Designs: Elevating Spaces, Enriching Lives

Embracing a guiding principle that masterfully intertwines usability, aesthetics, and economy, RnT Designs epitomises a seamless integration of form and function, elevating each creation to a harmonious symphony of design excellence. Their impressive background and technical proficiency enable them to offer comprehensive architectural services, catering to a diverse range of typologies with utmost finesse.

At the heart of their endeavour lies an unwavering dedication to a bespoke approach, recognizing the uniqueness of each project, encompassing size, budget, and constraints. Armed with consummate creative ability and technical prowess, RnT Designs embarks on a meticulously orchestrated five-step process -

from understanding client requirements to conceptual design, detailed development, integration of engineering principles, and culminating in project supervision and efficient execution.

The legacy of RnT Designs stands as a testament to their enduring commitment to shaping spaces that transcend expectations, encapsulating the essence of human experiences in tangible form. Within the fabric of this narrative, the reader embarks on a captivating journey of creation and innovation, immersed in the profound allure of architectural brilliance. Through the pages of this unfolding saga, the extraordinary vision and artistic finesse of RnT Designs illuminate the boundless possibilities that architecture holds, evoking admiration and awe in equal measure.

About Rashmi Mandal

With an extensive career spanning over 16 years, including a commendable 8-year tenure at Morphogenesis, Rashmi Mandal is a distinguished architectural expert. Her role has been marked by mentorship, team leadership, and relationship cultivation. A visionary, she spearheaded the establishment of a design firm, guided by her belief in architecture as multidisciplinary knowledge. Her design philosophy encompasses holistic spatial planning, uniting exterior and interior elements for optimal end-user experience, functionality, durability, and aesthetics. With a keen focus on sustainability, civil engineering, and emotional resonance, her designs harmoniously integrate purpose and surroundings, reflecting her profound architectural insight.

Prospects for Rashmi Mandal: RnT Designs

Collaborators for RnT Designs

- Real estate developers partnering to provide architectural and design services for projects.

- Construction companies collaborating to effectively implement architectural plans during construction.

- Sustainability organisations integrating eco-friendly elements into designs for sustainable practices.

- Non-profit organisations providing architectural services for community development and public spaces.

- Art and cultural institutions offering distinctive and immersive design concepts for museums and galleries.

Clients for RnT Designs

- Businesses in need of architectural and interior design solutions for their offices and retail spaces comprise the commercial clients seeking expert guidance.

- Homeowners looking to design or renovate their living spaces are residential clients seeking expert guidance and support.

- Real estate investors seeking expert guidance in ensuring their projects are well-designed and market-aligned.

Potential Investors for RnT Designs

- Private equity firms focusing on emerging firms in architectural design.

- Investors looking to support innovative ventures in the design sector.

- High net-worth individuals with a keen interest in design and real estate development.

Write to: rntdesigns.in@gmail.com

Bhavna Sresth

About Bhavna Sresth's Venture: Button Unbbutton

Button Unbbutton, established in 2022 under the visionary guidance of Bhavna Sresth, encapsulates a dynamic fusion of tradition and innovation. As a homegrown online brand, its core ethos revolves around harnessing the rich tapestry of Indian handlooms and infusing them into a contemporary fashion narrative. The brand emerges as a distinctive purveyor of style, catering to men and women of all age groups, creating a vibrant dialogue between heritage and modernity while championing the proud legacy of Indian culture.

Beyond its fashion offerings, Button Unbbutton stands as a conduit for unity and shared passion. With a resolute belief that the finest creations emerge from collective effort, the brand aspires to create a community that reveres and nurtures the ethos of handloom craftsmanship.

An embodiment of conscious sustainability, Button Unbbutton goes beyond being a brand and embraces a philosophy of reciprocity. It extends its care not only to its cherished patrons but also to the artisans whose skillful hands breathe life into each creation. This ethos lays the foundation for a harmonious ecosystem, bridging the gap between creator and consumer.

Button Unbbutton:
Weaving Heritage into Contemporary Fashion

Within this narrative, Button Unbbutton's essence manifests as a transformative platform, inviting all to revel in life's chromatic spectrum. Its contemporary styles, seamlessly interwoven with the intricate threads of Indian handlooms, curate a celebration of cultural vibrancy. A harmonious blend of tradition and modernity, the brand encapsulates the resplendent mosaic of India's heritage, portraying an elegant tapestry of expression.

In every garment, Button Unbbutton conveys not just a fashion statement but a poignant story that encapsulates the shared heritage and aspirations of its patrons. In this way, the brand aspires to become more than an emblem of style, positioning itself as a testament to the vivid hues that illuminate the journey of life.

About Bhavna Sresth

Bhavna Sresth's trajectory epitomises resilience and creative reawakening, tracing back to her father's pioneering legacy in textile design. From an early age, her affinity for colours and patterns blossomed in her father's atelier, instilling a profound creative essence. Navigating diverse paths including single parenthood and a stint in the entertainment industry, her creative flame endured. A 25-year tenure in Mumbai bore testament to her accomplishments, yet a latent dream resurfaced amid illness and the pandemic. Fueled by familial support and an unwavering vision, she now breathes life into her aspirations. Bhavna envisions beyond a brand, forging a community that reveres handlooms. Her designs eloquently echo India's heritage, where understated elegance converges with vibrancy. With humility, she embarks on this artistic voyage, extending an invitation to partake in her enchanting realm, seeking the collective embrace of support and appreciation.

Prospects for Bhavna Sresth: Button Unbbutton

Collaborators for Button Unbbutton

- Textile manufacturers looking to incorporate her design expertise into innovative textile products.

- Fashion brands wanting to partner with Bhavna to infuse culturally resonant designs into their collections.

- Handloom artisans showcasing traditional handloom skills through contemporary designs in collaboration with Bhavna.

- Retailers offering Bhavna's curated designs to their customer base and expanding their product range.

- Sustainable brands aligning with Bhavna's ethos to create eco-friendly and conscious fashion lines.

- Fashion institutes wanting to engage Bhavna as a guest lecturer or mentor to share her journey and insights with students.

- Event planners willing to collaborate with Bhavna to create bespoke textile and fashion pieces for special occasions.

- Online marketplaces featuring Bhavna's designs on e-commerce platforms to reach a global audience.

- Artists, photographers, and creative professionals interested in blending art and fashion in interdisciplinary projects collaborate on projects.

- Fashion influencer excited about showcasing Bhavna's creations to their followers, enhancing her brand visibility.

- Retail entrepreneurs considering Bhavna's designs for starting their own fashion retail businesses.

Clients for Button Unbbutton

- Individuals seeking unique and culturally resonant fashion designs.

- Fashion enthusiasts looking for sustainable and eco-friendly clothing options.

- Retailers and fashion boutiques interested in offering distinctive designs to their customers.

Potential Investors for Button Unbbutton

- Investors interested in the fashion, design and innovative ventures in the fashion sector.

- Private equity firms focusing on emerging fashion startups.

- High net-worth individuals with an affinity for the fashion and design industry.

Write to: buttonunbbutton@gmail.com

Meera Babu

About Meera Babu's Venture: Harmony Health Centre

Harmony Hearing Solution: Enriching Lives Through Sound

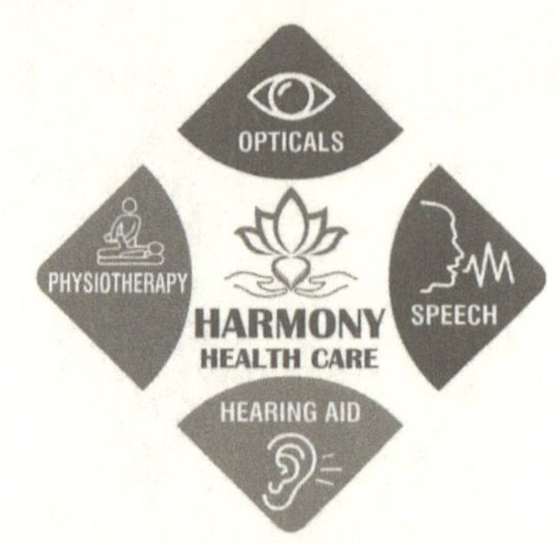

For over two decades, Venkateshwara Diagnostics Centre has been a beacon of comprehensive healthcare services, touching countless lives in Chennai. In a monumental stride forward, Director B. Meera has embarked on a new venture dedicated to hearing aids and ear care services, christened "Harmony Ear Care".

As an independent hearing instrument provider, Harmony Hearing Solution partners with Siemens Hearing Instruments to offer the latest advancements in hearing aid technology. Their vision is clear: to deliver the best possible hearing experience, tailored to each individual's unique needs, lifestyle, and budget. However, what sets them apart is their unwavering commitment to service. At Harmony Hearing Solution, your hearing is their priority. They strive to ensure your hearing aids are not just functional, but seamlessly integrated into your daily life.

Harmony Health Centre: Enriching Lives Through Sound

Harmony's dedicated team understands that hearing care is a deeply personal journey. They don't just treat symptoms; they strive to understand an individual, appreciating personal passions and recognizing what truly matters in a healthcare partner.

Harmony Hearing Solution offers a level of personalised care that stands unparalleled. They believe in creating a connection that goes beyond the technicalities of hearing aids and embraces the essence of you. This holistic approach to healthcare is what truly sets them apart.

Harmony Hearing Solution isn't just a name; it's a promise of harmony, balance, and an enriched auditory experience.

Commencing with hearing aid sales and services, Harmony Hearing Solution embarked on a transformative journey. Its growth unfolded across 3 branches, marking a notable 9-year legacy of service that has touched the lives of over 5000 individuals. Thriving in a niche industry, the demand for technical prowess became evident.

About Meera Babu

Meet Meera Babu, the visionary proprietor behind Harmony Hearing Solution, a venture that commenced its transformative journey in 2015. Despite her initial limited business knowledge, Meera's resolute determination and passion have guided the evolution of her enterprise. Remarkably, her personal journey with hearing challenges has provided her with a unique perspective, igniting her commitment to make a tangible difference in the lives of others facing similar hurdles.

Personally facing the challenges of hearing impairment, Meera's journey not only laid the foundation for Harmony Hearing Solution but also went through a notable evolution. Starting as Harmony Hearing Solution in 2015, it underwent a rebranding in 2021 to become Harmony Health Care, introducing a comprehensive array of services, encompassing Hearing Aid, Opticals, Physiotherapy, Speech Therapy, and Counseling Psychology. Guided by her own experiences, Meera ensures that each customer's journey is characterised by understanding, compassion, and precise solutions tailored to their needs.

Meera's legacy is not just one of business growth but also of profound impact. Through her endeavour, individuals not only regain their ability to hear but also reclaim their connection to life's vibrant symphony. Her journey exemplifies a remarkable fusion of personal experience, dedication, and entrepreneurial spirit, ultimately culminating in the creation of a space where hearing challenges are met with unwavering support and cutting-edge solutions.

Prospects for Meera Babu: Harmony Health Centre

Collaborators for Harmony Health Centre

- Meera seeks to establish connections with experienced professionals in healthcare, including physicians, specialists, nurses, and therapists. These partnerships will promote knowledge sharing and potential collaboration on healthcare initiatives.

- Meera aims to engage with healthcare service providers such as hospitals, clinics, diagnostic centres, and rehabilitation facilities. These connections will facilitate a comprehensive understanding of available services, creating opportunities for collaborative patient care.

- Meera is focused on forming strong affiliations with physicians across various medical disciplines. Through these partnerships, Meera aims to enhance patient outcomes, ensure evidence-based care, and contribute to a well-rounded healthcare approach.

Clients for Harmony Health Centre

- Individuals seeking high-quality, holistic healthcare services.

- Patients in need of specialised care and evidence-based treatment approaches.

Write to: meerababu1972@gmail.com

Prritii Shah

About Prritii Shah's Venture: Orga-Nichè

Orga-Nichè is intertwined with Prritii's deep-rooted exposure to the salon industry. Having witnessed firsthand the ramifications of hazardous chemicals on human

well-being, particularly their connection to carcinogenic risks, she felt a compelling need to reimagine the beauty industry. Orga-Nichè emerged as the embodiment of her vision – a beauty brand that harmonises with the environment and draws from the wisdom of nature.

Orga-Nichè is the exquisite tapestry where ancient wisdom elegantly intertwines with contemporary innovation. This harmonious blend gives birth to premium hair and skin care products that transcend gender and age, embracing the diverse needs of a modern, conscious audience.

> **Orga-Nichè:** Where Nature and Beauty Unite for Authentic Wellness

The heart of Orga-Nichè's distinctiveness lies in its multifaceted product range that transcends traditional beauty paradigms. Prritii's venture boldly embraces the broader spectrum of health and wellness, aligning with her holistic approach to beauty. This expansion amplifies Orga-Nichè's impact, transforming it from a beauty brand to a beacon of comprehensive well-being.

But Orga-Nichè's story doesn't end with products. It extends to a bespoke salon in Mumbai, where innovation and nature's bounty converge. This pioneering establishment pioneers the use of natural skin and hair products in a variety of services and live treatments, setting new standards for conscious beauty experiences.

Prritii Shah's venture, Orga-Nichè, emerges as a profound reflection of her values, beliefs, and personal journey. Every twist and turn of life has sculpted her into a passionate entrepreneur, one who understands that experiences and responses are the architects of personality. With an unwavering commitment to her convictions, Prritii has laid the very foundation of Orga-Nichè based on these principles.

The authenticity of Orga-Nichè is further underscored by its unwavering commitment to quality. Prritii ensures that every product carries the hallmarks of natural, organic, and vegan ingredients. Backed by certifications and licenses, Orga-Nichè's manufacturing facility is a testament to its dedication to purity and safety.

Orga-Nichè, under Prritii Shah's visionary leadership, emerges as a sanctuary where values, personal convictions, and entrepreneurial fervor converge. It's not just a business; it's a legacy of conscious living, a tribute to nature's abundance, and a catalyst for redefining the very essence of beauty and well-being.

About Prritii Shah

Prritii Shah's journey exemplifies not only her exceptional qualifications but also her immense potential as an entrepreneur and visionary. Armed with a solid educational foundation, including a graduation and an MBA in Finance from NMIMS, Prritii possesses the analytical acumen and strategic thinking that are essential in the business world. Her academic achievements are a testament to her dedication to learning and personal growth, showcasing her commitment to excellence from the outset.

Having delved into the realm of corporate finance and business advisory, Prritii's partnership role, where she managed finance and government liaising for a prominent builder, underlines her prowess in handling intricate financial matters and navigating complex regulatory landscapes. Her association with a marquee player in the industry is a testament to her skills and the level of trust her peers place in her capabilities. With an academic journey enriched by mastery in Neuro-Linguistic Programming (NLP), Prritii has cultivated extensive counseling expertise over the years, specializing in addressing the intricate relationship between mental health issues and their effects on skin, hair, and overall well-being.

Through her sharp wit and exceptional leadership abilities, the builder successfully secured the "L1" bid for a significant project within the state.

Prritii's journey doesn't just stop at her qualifications and corporate experience. It extends into the realm of resilience and adaptability. Her personal adventure in South Africa, coupled with the challenges of extricating herself from a toxic marriage, underscores her strength in the face of adversity. Her ability to emerge from these situations with grace and dignity speaks volumes about her emotional intelligence and her capacity to overcome obstacles with unwavering determination.

The launch and management of a successful salon business, followed by the inception of Orga-Nichè, reveal Prritii's innate entrepreneurial spirit and innovation. Her transition from a franchisee to the creator of a pioneering organic beauty brand highlights her capacity to envision and execute novel business concepts. In the face of financial setbacks and a global pandemic, her perseverance shines through, showcasing her tenacity and ability to navigate challenging environments.

Prritii's choice to create Orga-Nichè as a manifestation of her values and passion for natural beauty is a testament to her foresight and understanding of market trends. The brand's unique proposition, including its emphasis on health and wellness, showcases her ability to identify and seize opportunities that go beyond conventional boundaries.

Prospects for Prritii Shah: Orga-Nichè

Collaborators for Orga-Nichè

- Orga-Nichè seeks collaborators passionate about natural beauty, wellness, and innovative entrepreneurship.

- Opportunity for beauty and wellness professionals to join as new branches open in Tier-I Indian cities.

- Collaborators who aim for exceptional experiences that aligns with her brands focus on organic and safe beauty.

- The brand welcomes salon experts and holistic practitioners to embark on a journey redefining beauty.

Clients for Orga-Nichè

- Eco-conscious consumers prioritise natural, organic, and vegan products in their beauty and wellness routines. They are likely to be environmentally aware and seek products that align with their values.

- Salon owners and stylists who are looking to incorporate natural and organic products into their services. They value quality and are interested in offering a unique and conscious experience to their clients.

- Health and wellness spas focus on holistic well-being and aim to provide services using natural and organic products. They seek premium, high-quality products that enhance their offerings and resonate with their clientele.

- Businesses that specialise in offering niche and high-end beauty products. They are likely to appreciate Orga-Nichè's commitment to quality, authenticity, and its unique position in the market.

- Influencers and content creators in the health, wellness, and beauty space who advocate for natural and sustainable products. They have a dedicated following interested in conscious living and are potential advocates for Orga-Nichè.

Investors for Orga-Nichè

- Socially-conscious impact investors.

- Angel investors with a focus on sustainable ventures.

- Private equity firms specializing in beauty and wellness.

- High net-worth individuals with a passion for conscious beauty.

- Investment groups focused on consumer goods.

- Angel investors with expertise in health and wellness.

- Impact investing networks.

- Family offices with a focus on sustainable ventures.

Write to: prritiishah05@gmail.com

Dharini R

About Dharini R's Venture:
ARDE Interactive Pvt. Ltd.

ARDE Interactive Pvt. Ltd. sets itself apart as a trailblazer with a mission: to provide customised, market-ready, consumer-centric digital solutions across diverse industries. Their primary objective is to empower businesses spanning various sectors with state-of-the-art technology and digital strategies meticulously tailored to their unique needs.

At the heart of ARDE's approach lies the corporate retainer service model, ensuring a recurring revenue stream. With a remarkable 15-year industry experience, they have solidified their status as a prominent player, serving a myriad of global corporations and businesses. ARDE's distinctiveness is rooted in their unwavering commitment to comprehending the distinct requirements of each client. By intently listening to their clients' needs, they engineer solutions that yield exceptional results.

> **ARDE:** Leading the Way in Tailored Digital Solutions for Empowered Businesses

Quality is the bedrock of ARDE's ethos. Their team of experts leaves no stone unturned in delivering products and services that meet the highest industry standards. A distinguishing feature is their knack for timely execution, acknowledging its paramount importance in today's fast-paced business landscape.

In an environment where exceeding expectations is imperative, ARDE consistently rises above. Their steadfast commitment to excellence renders them the preferred choice for businesses seeking reliable, top-notch solutions to propel their digital journey. ARDE isn't just a venture; it represents empowerment and transformation for businesses venturing into the digital realm.

About Dharini R

Dharini R, the driving force behind ARDE Interactive Pvt. Ltd., embarked on her entrepreneurial journey with a simple yet powerful motive – to bridge the market gap. Recognizing the need for personalised digital solutions for diverse businesses, she understood that success in the digital world required more than just technology.

Dharini's vision is crystal clear – to empower businesses with digital tools tailored to their needs. Staying updated on tech trends, ARDE Interactive Pvt. Ltd. under her leadership delivers cutting-edge solutions to clients.

Looking ahead, Dharini envisions a future where ARDE Interactive Pvt. Ltd. offers a full spectrum of digital services, guiding businesses through their online journey with innovation.

Her primary income strategy relies on a retainer model, ensuring financial stability. As she navigates expansion, Dharini seeks partnerships with experts, investors, and industry leaders who share her vision of technology-enabled business empowerment.

With a legacy of 15+ years, Dharini has emerged as a trailblazer. Her unique ability to grasp each business's distinct needs and craft tailor-made solutions sets her apart. Quality and punctuality are her hallmarks. Dharini's journey is a testament to her dedication to helping businesses thrive in the digital age, an ongoing story of inspiration and transformation.

Prospects for Dharini R: ARDE Interactive Pvt. Ltd.

Collaborators for ARDE Interactive Pvt. Ltd.

- Companies specializing in complementary technologies that can be integrated with ARDE's solutions to enhance their offerings.

- Experts in various industries who can provide valuable insights and domain knowledge to help ARDE tailor their solutions to meet specific sector needs.

- Collaborating with agencies that specialise in digital marketing can complement ARDE's services, providing a comprehensive digital transformation package for clients.

- Partnerships with firms specializing in software development can enhance ARDE's capacity to deliver customised solutions to their clients.

- Collaborating with large multinational corporations that operate across various industries could lead to mutually beneficial projects and long-term partnerships.

- Partnering with universities and research institutions can open avenues for innovation and development of cutting-edge technologies and strategies.

- Partnering with cloud service providers can offer ARDE the infrastructure and scalability needed for their digital solutions.

- Joining forces with industry associations can help ARDE gain visibility and access to a network of potential clients and collaborators.

- Teaming up with UX design experts can enhance the user-centric aspect of ARDE's digital solutions, ensuring a seamless experience for end-users.

Clients for ARDE Interactive Pvt. Ltd.

- Businesses seeking comprehensive end-to-end digital solutions.

- Companies looking to adapt seamlessly to the evolving market landscape.

- Organisations in need of innovative and tailored digital strategies.

- Entities navigating the competitive digital era and looking for a reliable technology partner.

- Enterprises aiming to tackle challenges and seize opportunities in the dynamic digital environment.

Potential Investors for ARDE Interactive Pvt. Ltd.

- Individual angel investors and corporate with a passion for technology and digital solutions are encouraged to apply. Join ARDE in our journey to revolutionise the digital landscape.

- Investment groups with a focus on technology companies are encouraged to apply. Join hands with ARDE and be part of the digital transformation journey.

- Companies or individuals with a strategic interest in ARDE's offerings are invited for collaboration.

Write to: dharini.r@ardeint.com

Deepal Mistry

About Deepal Mistry's Venture: Ascent Insights

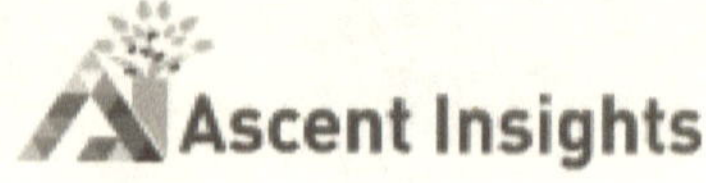

Ascent Insights is a pioneering force in the pharmaceutical industry, offering strategic consultation and brand/product life-cycle management services that empower businesses to excel in a rapidly evolving landscape. With a focus on precision and innovation, they are proud partners to a diverse portfolio of multinational corporations (MNCs) and prominent Indian pharmaceutical houses. They hold the privilege of managing some of India's most renowned pharmaceutical brands, meticulously shaping their strategies and tactics for enduring success. Their primary revenue model revolves around strategic consultation, where their seasoned experts collaborate closely with clients to craft customised strategies aligned with their unique objectives, providing invaluable insights to navigate challenges and capitalise on opportunities. Additionally, they specialise in optimizing product portfolios, extending product life-cycles, and making informed decisions regarding product launches and market positioning.

Ascent Insights: Pioneering AI-driven Solutions for a Transformative Future.

Beyond conventional practices, they are experts in suggesting innovative interventions in the patient journey, leveraging digital technologies to enhance patient experiences and engagement. Their collaborative partnerships with industry leaders keep them at the forefront of emerging trends and best practices, ensuring that they offer their clients the latest insights and innovations. At Ascent Insights, the vision is a future where pharmaceutical excellence is the norm, and they are steadfast in their mission to guide their clients towards this aspirational peak.

Tailored Business Strategies for Pharmaceutical Industry

Ascent Insights specialises in crafting customised business strategies for clients in the pharmaceutical industry. Their approach involves a deep comprehension of each client's specific objectives and challenges, resulting in strategies precisely aligned with their unique needs.

Portfolio Enhancement

A fundamental strategic focus is on optimizing product portfolios and extending product life-cycles. This entails thorough evaluation of market dynamics, competition, and consumer preferences to ensure that client products remain relevant and profitable.

Market Positioning

They provide expert guidance on market positioning. Through in-depth market analysis, they assist clients in making well-informed decisions about product launches and how to effectively position their brands to gain a competitive edge.

Vision for Excellence

The overarching vision of Ascent Insights is to elevate businesses and brands to new heights of excellence. Their commitment to innovation, precision, and strategic thinking underpins their mission to guide clients towards enduring success.

About Deepal Mistry

Deepal Mistry stands as a luminary in the world of entrepreneurship, renowned for her visionary leadership and unwavering commitment to business innovation. With a rich family history steeped in commerce, Deepal's entrepreneurial spirit has been honed over the years, leading her to significant achievements in the corporate world and beyond.

As the Founder of 'Ascent Insights,' Deepal has demonstrated a remarkable ability to envision the future of business. Under her guidance, Ascent Insights seamlessly integrates technology, human intelligence, and artificial intelligence to empower businesses and drive growth. The company offers a diverse range of solutions, including business management, phygital branding, and communications, all designed to meet the evolving needs of the business landscape.

Deepal's entrepreneurial journey has been marked by relentless dedication to sustainability, innovative thinking, and a deep understanding of consumer behavior. Her invaluable insights and expertise have been instrumental in propelling brands from their infancy to remarkable market success.

With a career spanning over 22 years, Deepal embodies the core values of insights, innovation, consistency, and commitment, which have been fundamental to the accomplishments of Ascent Insights. Her guidance and leadership are not only shaping the present but also driving businesses into a tech-savvy and dynamic future, where human intelligence and artificial intelligence work harmoniously to achieve unparalleled success.

Prospects for Deepal Mistry: Ascent Insights

Collaborators for Ascent Insights

- Companies specializing in healthcare technology can enhance patient experiences and engagement through innovative digital solutions.

- Research institutions can benefit from Ascent Insights' strategic expertise to develop and implement cutting-edge approaches based on the latest research.

- Collaborating with market research firms can provide Ascent Insights with valuable data and insights to inform their strategic recommendations.

- Experts in regulatory compliance can ensure that Ascent Insights' strategies align with industry standards and regulatory requirements.

- Consulting firms specializing in healthcare can enhance their offerings by partnering with Ascent Insights to provide specialised services in the pharmaceutical sector.

- Associations and conferences in the medical field can benefit from Ascent Insights' expertise, gaining valuable insights and strategies to share with their members.

- Academic consultants can contribute specialised knowledge and insights to the development of tailored strategies for pharmaceutical clients.

- Experts in supply chain and distribution can collaborate with Ascent Insights to optimise product portfolios and extend product life-cycles.

- Patient advocacy groups can provide valuable insights into patient perspectives and needs, allowing Ascent Insights to develop more patient-centric strategies.

- Consulting firms specializing in life sciences can find synergies in providing comprehensive services to clients in the pharmaceutical industry by collaborating with Ascent Insights.

Clients for Ascent Insights

- Large global pharmaceutical companies seeking strategic consultation and brand/product life-cycle management services to excel in the evolving pharmaceutical landscape.

- Established Indian pharmaceutical companies looking to enhance their strategies and tactics for enduring success, as well as managing renowned pharmaceutical brands effectively.

- Smaller or newer pharmaceutical companies looking for expert guidance in navigating the competitive landscape, optimizing their product portfolios, and gaining a competitive edge through effective market positioning.

- Professionals responsible for overseeing and managing the brands of pharmaceutical products, seeking tailored strategies and consultation to enhance brand performance and market presence.

- Individuals responsible for product management and marketing within pharmaceutical companies, looking for specialised insights to extend product life-cycles and make informed decisions regarding product launches.

- Companies in the healthcare technology sector interested in innovative interventions in the patient journey, leveraging digital technologies to enhance patient experiences and engagement.

- Organisations representing the pharmaceutical industry seeking strategic consultation and insights to benefit their member companies and advance the industry as a whole.

- Entities responsible for regulating and overseeing pharmaceutical products and practices, looking for expert guidance and consultation to enhance industry standards and practices.

- Consulting firms specializing in healthcare seeking partnership or collaboration with Ascent Insights to offer specialised services in the pharmaceutical sector.

Potential Investors for Ascent Insights

- A VC firm with a strong track record in funding innovative companies in the healthcare and technology sectors.

- An investor or investment group with expertise in pharmaceuticals and a keen interest in supporting consultancy services.

- A large corporation with a presence in healthcare or technology, looking to expand its offerings or collaborate with innovative startups.

- A firm with a history of investing in life sciences companies that demonstrate high potential for innovation and growth.

- An impact investor seeking to support companies that not only promise financial returns but also have a positive societal impact, particularly in the healthcare sector.

In the world of AI, the convergence of collaborators, clients, and investors forms a powerful ecosystem propelling Ascent Insights towards its mission of unlocking AI's full potential in healthcare and beyond. Together, these stakeholders pave the way for a future where AI-driven solutions are not just possibilities but tangible realities waiting to be realised.

Write to: <u>Deepal.mistry@ascentinsightsglobal.com</u>

Veena Venkataraman

About Veena Venkataraman's Venture:
Sanskruthi Shlokalaya

Sanskruthi Shlokalaya, envisioned by Veena Venkatraman, stands as an inspiring beacon of positivity and learning for children aged 2.5 years and older, nurturing their understanding of cultural roots and values. This vibrant initiative is an immersive journey into the world of deities, shlokas, storytelling, and engaging activities. Through the tales and teachings from mythology and puranas, children not only gain meaningful awareness but also develop increased confidence, positivity, and a deeper connection with their cultural heritage.

Sanskruthi Shlokalaya's journey, which began with a small group called the Lamb Tail Club, has evolved significantly. It now caters to kids globally through various batches, even accommodating early morning sessions to suit different time zones. The concept has grown into Sanskruthi Shlokalaya, with an extensive curriculum, interactive binders, and adult shloka chanting classes. Additionally, Sanskruthi Shlokalaya has expanded its offerings to include props and products related to the stories, reinforcing the teachings.

Sanskruthi Shlokalaya: Cultivating Values Through Chanting and Puranas

Recognised for its outstanding contributions, Sanskruthi Shlokalaya and Veena Venkatraman have earned several accolades and awards, such as the Best Educator at the SHE Awards 2022 and the Big Red National Level Entrepreneur Award 2022 for Best Sloka Instructor of the Year. Through testimonies of students and parents alike, it is evident that Sanskruthi Shlokalaya has made a significant impact on young minds, fostering a love for culture, mythology, and spirituality while promoting overall well-being. Veena's unique approach to teaching shlokas has garnered admiration, ensuring that the next generation cherishes its heritage with enthusiasm and positivity.

About Veena

Veena Venkatraman, a visionary leader with a background in BE Industrial Engineering and certified as a Vedic Heritage Coach, is the driving force behind Sanskruthi Shlokalaya. Her unique blend of industrial engineering knowledge with a deep understanding of Vedic heritage allows her to offer a holistic approach to education and well-being.

At Sanskruthi Shlokalaya, Veena's mission is clear: to impart a sense of serenity and compassion in young minds through the practice of pranayama and Shloka chanting. By introducing these ancient practices at a young age, she aims to foster resilience and promote overall well-being in children.

Beyond education, Veena is adept at harmoniously combining the pursuit of knowledge with revenue generation at Sanskruthi Shlokalaya. Her commitment to this mission is paralleled by her efforts in establishing meaningful connections with parents, pre-schools, and women's collectives who resonate with her vision of nurturing values and preserving cultural heritage for the younger generation. Veena Venkatraman is the visionary leader behind Sanskruthi Shlokalaya, a beacon of wisdom and tranquility in a fast-paced world. Her mission is to instill a sense of calmness and compassion in young minds through pranayama and Shloka chanting, promoting resilience and well-being from a tender age.

Prospects for Veena Venkataraman: Sanskruthi Shlokalaya

Collaborators for Sanskruthi Shlokalaya

- Yoga instructors and studios specializing in pranayama and meditation, who can complement Shlokalaya's offerings by providing physical practices to enhance holistic well-being.

- Experts in Sanskrit language and literature who can contribute to the depth and authenticity of shloka chanting sessions.

- Coaches and practitioners who specialise in mindfulness and meditation techniques, providing additional tools for emotional and mental well-being.

- Professionals with expertise in early childhood education who understand the benefits of incorporating mindfulness practices for young learners.

- Organisations dedicated to preserving and promoting cultural heritage, who can collaborate with Shlokalaya to integrate traditional practices into educational programs.

- Licensed professionals specializing in child psychology and mental health, who can provide valuable insights on the benefits of mindfulness practices for children.

- Developers of educational apps or platforms that can complement Shlokalaya's offerings by providing interactive tools for learning and practice.

- Coaches and experts in parenting techniques who can collaborate with Shlokalaya to offer a comprehensive approach to holistic parenting.

- Instructors in creative arts like painting, music, or dance, who can integrate their expertise with Shloka chanting for a well-rounded educational experience.

- Community centres or wellness facilities interested in offering holistic educational programs to their members or clients.

Clients for Sanskruthi Shlokalaya

- Parents who value a holistic approach to education that includes practices like pranayama and shloka chanting for their children.

- Educational institutions focused on early childhood development that recognise the value of incorporating ancient practices into their curriculum.

- Groups and organisations dedicated to preserving cultural heritage and values, particularly those interested in imparting this knowledge to the younger generation.

- Individuals or groups passionate about innovative educational approaches and the integration of traditional practices in modern learning environments.

- Centres that offer programs or services focused on mental and emotional well-being, who may see value in incorporating pranayama and shloka chanting.

- Individuals or groups interested in preserving and promoting vedic heritage and its practices, particularly in the context of education.

- Organisers of events and gatherings centred around cultural enrichment and education, who may be interested in featuring Sanskruthi Shlokalaya's offerings.

- Professionals in the education sector who see the potential value of integrating practices like Pranayama and shloka chanting in educational settings.

- Experts in child psychology, development, and well-being who understand the benefits of incorporating mindfulness practices in early education.

- Professionals in the field of holistic health and wellness who recognise the importance of mental and emotional well-being in overall health.

Potential Investors for Sanskruthi Shlokalaya

- Investors who specialise in funding ventures related to wellness, holistic health, and mindfulness practices.

- Investors interested in innovative educational approaches and technologies that enhance learning experiences.

- Funds or investors dedicated to preserving and promoting cultural heritage and traditions.

- Investors seeking opportunities that not only promise financial returns but also have a positive societal impact, particularly in the realm of holistic education.

- Individual investors who are passionate about supporting innovative educational initiatives and startups.

- Philanthropic foundations, with a mission to support initiatives related to education, well-being, and cultural preservation.

- Investors with a background or interest in the yoga and mindfulness industry, who understand the value of practices like pranayama and shloka chanting.

- Investors who prioritise projects and initiatives that align with their values of social impact and community well-being.

Write to: veenavkesh@gmail.com

Padmapriyadharsini

About Padmapriyadharsini's Venture: Yogatathva (*A Centre of Excellence*)

Established in 2015, Yogatathva epitomises Padma's vision to integrate therapeutic yoga into healthcare seamlessly. Backed by over 11 years of experience, extensive expertise, and dedicated research, Padmapriyadharsini has solidified Yogatathva's position as a hub of excellence. It serves as a sanctuary where individuals can access tailored yoga therapy solutions to address a diverse range of health concerns.

Yogatathva's offerings encompass bespoke yoga therapy, expert consultations, corporate wellness programs, pre/postnatal pregnancy therapy, and the alleviation of issues such as pain management, stress mitigation, insomnia, and more. The centre specialises in delivering remedies for acute and chronic conditions, all aimed at elevating the holistic well-being of its clientele.

> **Yogatathva:** Transforming Lives through Therapeutic Yoga

Yogatathva is a Therapeutic Yoga Wellness Centre spearheaded by Padmapriyadharsini, a highly credentialed Yoga Therapist with extensive proficiency in the domain. Possessing qualifications including an MSc., MD(ACU), 500 HRS Aadhi Yoga certification, recognition as a Yoga Therapy Expert by AYUSH, and membership in the International Yoga Alliance, Padmapriyadharsini is devoted to furnishing personalised yoga therapy solutions to individuals seeking holistic health and wellness.

Yogatathva extends a wide spectrum of services, both online and offline. The centre specialises in furnishing yoga therapy solutions for both acute and chronic conditions, with the ultimate goal of enhancing the overall well-being of its patrons.

Yogatathva boasts a track record of successful outcomes, with individuals reaping the benefits of its therapy sessions. From surmounting challenges like heart blocks and weight loss to managing insomnia and stress, the centre's therapy sessions have left a positive imprint on the lives of numerous individuals. Corporate packages, ongoing yoga sessions, workshops, and challenges are also integral components of Yogatathva's offerings, rendering it accessible to a diverse clientele, encompassing corporations, hospitals, organisations, and educational institutions.

The centre's accomplishments and course offerings bear testament to its dedication to advocating yoga as a therapeutic discipline. With a steadfast focus on holistic health, Yogatathva aspires to aid individuals in attaining equilibrium and serenity in their lives through the practice of yoga and mindfulness. Whether it's relief from stress, management of pain, or the pursuit of overall well-being, Yogatathva is resolutely committed to accompanying clients on their voyage towards a state of optimal health and well-being.

- Corporate clientele, including companies like YAMAHA, FIDELITY, HP, NETMEDS, TANISH, and MARKETSIMPLIFIED, benefit from customised well-being programs for their employees.

About Padmapriyadharsini

Padmapriyadharsini, an accomplished Yoga Therapist and the Founder of Yogatathva, is a visionary leader dedicated to promoting therapeutic yoga practices globally. With a profound commitment to wellness, her journey has been marked by exceptional achievements and a relentless pursuit of her mission to bring the benefits of yoga to millions of people worldwide.

Padmapriyadharsini's educational background is impressive, with a B.Tech in IT from Anna University Chennai and an MD in Acupuncture from Bharathiar University. Her quest for knowledge and expertise extends further with qualifications such as M.Sc. in Yoga Therapy, International Registered Yoga Therapist with Yoga Alliance, Certified 500 TTC Yoga Instructor (Aadhi Yoga), International Fitness Zumba Instructor, International ZIN Kids Specialist Instructor, International CAD Certified Instructor, Certified Specialist in Food, Naturopathy Therapy, Certified Specialist in Sujok Pain Management, Certified Acupuncture & Acupressure Therapist, International Certified Aerial Yoga Instructor, and AYUSH Ministry Certified Yoga Therapist. Her dedication to continuous learning and specialization sets her apart as a leading authority in the field of yoga therapy.

Padmapriyadharsini's notable awards and recognitions, including the Visionary Women Award, She Asia's Iconic Yoga Therapist Award, NOBLE GOLDEN CROWN AWARD for Best Yoga Therapist, and SIWAA AWARD for Outstanding Women Entrepreneur, underscore her exceptional contributions to the field of yoga therapy.

Her vision for the future is grounded in collaboration, particularly with specialists in the Prevention of Sexual Harassment (POSH) and the impending Private Mediation Bill. Additionally, she is committed to offering consultation services to junior lawyers, furthering her mission to create a more equitable society where justice and wellness prevail for all. Padmapriyadharsini's journey is a testament to her unwavering dedication to the art and science of yoga therapy and its transformative potential in promoting holistic health and well-being.

Prospects For Padmapriyadharshini: Yogatathva

Collaborators for Yogatathva

- Collaborating with local yoga studios and instructors can expand Yogatathva's reach and provide additional venues for offering yoga therapy sessions.

- Partnering with retreat centres that focus on holistic health and well-being can lead to joint events or specialised retreats combining yoga therapy with other wellness practices.

- Collaborating with medical professionals, such as physiotherapists, chiropractors, or pain management specialists, can offer complementary approaches to patient care.

- Collaborating with nutrition experts can provide a comprehensive approach to holistic health by incorporating dietary recommendations along with yoga therapy.

- Partnering with instructors who specialise in mindfulness and meditation can enhance the mental and emotional well-being aspect of holistic health.

- Collaborating with practitioners in alternative therapies like acupuncture, Ayurveda, or naturopathy can offer clients a well-rounded approach to health and wellness.

- Partnering with fitness trainers and exercise instructors can complement yoga therapy with tailored physical fitness programs for clients.

- Collaborating with companies that develop wellness apps or technology solutions can offer clients additional resources for practicing yoga therapy at home.

- Partnering with schools or educational institutions to offer yoga therapy programs for students can promote holistic well-being from a young age.

- Collaborating with retreat centres focused on holistic health and well-being can lead to joint programs and events that benefit both organisations.

- Partnering with psychologists, therapists, and counselors can provide a comprehensive approach to mental health and emotional well-being through yoga therapy. Vision for partnerships, especially in matters related to the Prevention of Sexual Harassment (POSH).

- Collaborating with companies that produce wellness products, such as meditation cushions or yoga props, can provide clients with additional resources for their practice.

Clients for Yogatathva

- Individuals looking for personalised yoga therapy solutions to address specific health concerns such as pain management, stress, insomnia, and chronic conditions.

- Companies interested in providing wellness programs for their employees, including tailored yoga therapy sessions and stress management programs.

- Healthcare institutions looking to complement their medical services with holistic therapies for patients dealing with chronic conditions or seeking alternative health solutions.

- Women in various stages of pregnancy seeking specialised yoga therapy to support their physical and mental well-being during and after pregnancy.

- Educational institutions, interested in incorporating yoga therapy as part of their wellness programs for students and faculty members.

- Wellness centres looking to expand their range of services by including yoga therapy as an option for clients seeking holistic health solutions.

- Groups or organisations dedicated to promoting stress management and overall well-being, who may benefit from Yogatathva's expertise in providing tailored solutions.

- Practitioners in the holistic health field who may want to collaborate with Yogatathva to offer complementary therapies to their clients.

- Individuals with acute or chronic health conditions such as pain, insomnia, anxiety, and stress, seeking holistic approaches for relief and management.

- Individuals who are passionate about maintaining overall health and well-being and are interested in exploring yoga therapy as part of their wellness routine.

Potential Investors for Yogatathva

- Individuals or organisations interested in supporting the growth and expansion of the wellness centre.

- Investors who believe in the transformative power of yoga therapy and personalised well-being journeys.

- Opportunity to contribute to the promotion of holistic health and wellness.

Write to: yogatathva@gmail.com

Harini Nischal

About Harini Nischal's Venture: Harini Designs

Harini Nischal, the visionary force behind Harini Designs, is a luminary in the realm of Indian craftsmanship and design sensibilities. With an illustrious career spanning over two decades, she stands as a torchbearer of India's rich heritage, particularly in the domain of

Andhra handlooms. Her journey is a testament to an unwavering passion for preserving and reimagining the nation's artistic treasures.

Born and raised in the heartland of Andhra Pradesh, Harini's affinity for Andhra Handlooms is deeply rooted in her cultural heritage. This intrinsic love for indigenous textiles forms the very foundation of her brand, Harini Designs. Through her artistic prowess, Harini seamlessly blends contemporary aesthetics with intricate traditional craftsmanship, creating designs that transcend time.

> **Harini Nischal:**
> Weaving Traditions into Contemporary Elegance

Harini's expertise in the delicate crafts of stitching and tailoring, coupled with her keen fashion sensibilities, allows her to craft pieces that effortlessly bridge the gap between tradition and modernity. This unique ability is what sets her creations apart, making them a cherished choice for the modern woman who appreciates the elegance of bespoke wardrobe selections.

Inclusivity lies at the core of Harini's creations. Her designs are thoughtfully curated to cater to a diverse range of sizes, reflecting her belief that fashion should be accessible to individuals from all walks of life. The earthy hues that permeate her collections resonate universally, adding a touch of timeless grace to each piece.

Beyond being an accomplished designer and entrepreneur, Harini Nischal is also an educator. Her tenure as a fashion faculty member for a decade in IITC for CAD underscores her commitment to nurturing the next generation of design enthusiasts.

Harini envisions her artistic pieces as more than mere fashion; they are essential components of a woman's collection, perfect for gifting, and suitable for women of all ages. Her brand, Harini Designs, encapsulates the essence of Indian heritage reimagined for the discerning contemporary woman.

Harini Designs: Bridging Tradition and Modernity

Harini Designs, under the visionary leadership of B. Harini Nischal, stands as a beacon of Indian craftsmanship harmoniously blended with contemporary design sensibilities. For over two decades, the brand has been a torchbearer of India's rich textile heritage, particularly through the innovative use of Andhra handloom textiles.

The offerings of Harini Designs are a testament to the enduring charm of traditional Indian craftsmanship reimagined for the modern woman. Each piece reflects a deep commitment to preserving the nation's artistic treasures, offering a captivating array of charms tailored for Indian women who value elegant and meticulously crafted wardrobe choices.

The brand's innovative use of Andhra handloom textiles in contemporary styles adds an extra layer of sophistication to its offerings. This unique fusion of tradition and modernity is what sets Harini Designs apart, making it a go-to choice for women who appreciate the timeless allure of bespoke fashion.

Harini Nischal's vision for her brand extends beyond fashion; it is a celebration of the essence of Indian heritage, woven into every thread and design. Her creations stand as essential components of every woman's collection, perfect for gifting, and suitable for women of all ages. Harini Designs is not just a brand; it is a testament to the enduring beauty of Indian craftsmanship in the modern world.

Prospects for Harini Nischal: Harini Designs

Collaborators for Harini Designs

- Collaborating with skilled artisans and craftsmen who specialise in traditional Indian craftsmanship to create unique designs.

- Partnering with suppliers and weavers of Indian textiles, especially those specializing in Andhra handlooms, to source high-quality materials for designs.

- Collaborating with fashion retailers and boutiques to feature Harini Designs as part of their curated collections.

- Partnering with event and wedding planners to provide custom-designed outfits for brides, bridal parties, and attendees.

- Collaborating with fashion design schools for workshops, mentorship programs, or guest lectures to inspire and nurture emerging talent.

- Partnering with online platforms to showcase and sell Harini Designs' creations to a wider audience.

- Participating in art and craft exhibitions and fairs to showcase and sell Harini Designs' unique creations to a diverse audience.

- Collaborating with fashion bloggers and influencers for product reviews, styling tips, and features to increase brand visibility.

- Partnering with photographers and stylists for fashion shoots and editorial features to showcase Harini Designs in a visually appealing manner.

- Collaborating with jewelry designers to create coordinated ensembles that complement both the clothing and accessories.

- Partnering with organisations focused on preserving and promoting Indian art and culture for events, exhibitions, or cultural showcases.

- Participating in fashion events and shows to showcase Harini Designs' creations on a larger platform and connect with potential clients and collaborators.

- Collaborating with brands that share similar values in promoting ethical and sustainable fashion practices.

Clients for Harini Designs

- Individuals who have a keen interest in fashion and appreciate unique, bespoke wardrobe choices.

- Women who value elegance, sophistication, and meticulously crafted clothing options for various occasions.

- Individuals who have an appreciation for traditional craftsmanship and artistic forms blended with contemporary design sensibilities.

- Individuals who appreciate and seek out clothing made from traditional Indian textiles, especially those with an affinity for Andhra handlooms.

- Individuals who prefer personalised, made-to-order clothing options that reflect their unique style and preferences.

- Women of various body types and sizes who appreciate inclusivity in fashion and are looking for clothing options that cater to their specific needs.

- Individuals looking for special, thoughtful gifts for loved ones, particularly women who appreciate timeless and elegant fashion choices.

- Brides and bridal parties seeking bespoke, intricately designed outfits for weddings and related events.

- Women in professional settings who value sophisticated, well-crafted attire for the workplace.

- Boutiques and stores that specialise in curating unique, handcrafted fashion and accessories, and are interested in featuring Harini Designs.

- Individuals attending cultural events, festivals, or special occasions who seek culturally-inspired clothing choices that blend tradition with contemporary style.

Potential Investors for Harini Designs

- Individuals or firms with a background or interest in investing in fashion-related businesses. They may see potential in the unique blend of traditional Indian craftsmanship and contemporary design offered by Harini Designs.

- Investors with a focus on textiles and related industries may be interested in supporting a brand like Harini Designs, which places a strong emphasis on utilizing Indian textiles, especially Andhra handlooms.

- *Angel* investors who have a passion for art, crafts, and preserving cultural heritage may see the value in supporting a brand like Harini Designs that is deeply rooted in Indian craftsmanship.

- Investors who prioritise ethical and sustainable fashion practices may be attracted to Harini Designs' commitment to preserving traditional crafts and using eco-friendly materials.

- Investors who value the preservation and promotion of cultural heritage may be inclined to invest in a brand like Harini Designs, which places a strong emphasis on traditional Indian craftsmanship.

- Individuals with a high net-worth who have a personal interest in fashion and appreciate unique, bespoke wardrobe choices may see value in investing in Harini Designs.

- Impact investors who seek to make a positive social or environmental impact through their investments may be attracted to Harini Designs' commitment to preserving traditional crafts and supporting artisans.

- Utilizing crowd-funding platforms that focus on fashion and artisanal products may be another avenue for attracting investors who believe in the mission and vision of Harini Designs.

Write to: Desbiz7@gmail.com

Priya Nazareth

About Priya Nazareth's Venture: Monsher India Safety Equipments Pvt. Ltd.

Monsher India Safety Equipments Pvt. Ltd., stands as a formidable presence in the Indian fire and security industry, operating under the esteemed Monsher Fire Protection group. With an illustrious legacy spanning over five decades, this subsidiary shines as a beacon of excellence in the realm of safety solutions. Monsher India Safety Equipments occupies a central role within the Monsher Fire Protection conglomerate, which comprises three distinct entities: Monsher Protection (Projects), Monsher India Safety Equipments (Products), and Monsher Fire Controls (After Sales Service).

The subsidiary's hallmark strength is its comprehensive approach, positioning itself as the quintessential one-stop destination for a broad spectrum of fire and security needs.

> **Monsher India Safety Equipments Pvt. Ltd.:** Your Trusted Partner for Integrated Fire and Security Solutions

It prides itself on an impressive portfolio encompassing an array of cutting-edge products and services, underlining its steadfast commitment to delivering holistic safety solutions.

In a remarkable feat, Monsher India Safety Equipments Pvt. Ltd., has expanded its reach exponentially within a mere three years since its inception. This expansion entailed the strategic establishment of branch offices and state-of-the-art warehouses across key locations in India, including Hyderabad, Bangalore, Chennai, Kochi, and Delhi. These well-positioned facilities have allowed the company to efficiently cater to its growing clientele, further cementing its reputation as a reliable and efficient provider of top-tier fire and security solutions. Notably, the company has actively participated in major infrastructure projects across Mumbai, forged collaborations with six international firms for the manufacturing of premium fire and security equipment, and earned the coveted approval of prominent consultants and clients throughout India. Monsher India Safety Equipments Pvt. Ltd., continues to lead the charge in ensuring the safety and security of diverse clients across the nation, setting new standards of excellence along the way.

About Priya Nazareth

Priya Nazareth has embarked on an extraordinary journey as the Director of Monsher India Safety Equipments Pvt. Ltd. Her professional path took shape initially as a design expert collaborating with prestigious advertising agencies and production houses. However, Priya's career trajectory underwent a significant shift when she ventured into the dynamic realm of Fire and Security.

Two decades ago, Priya Nazareth assumed a pivotal role in pioneering the products division of Monsher. Her vision, leadership, and unwavering commitment have played an instrumental role in steering the company towards remarkable growth and expansion. Her tenure as Director has witnessed the introduction of innovative safety solutions, making Monsher a trailblazer in the industry.

At the heart of Priya's mission is a profound commitment to enhancing safety in all human spaces. She envisions a world where user-friendly fire-fighting equipment is readily available to protect lives and property. This vision materialised in the form of Monsher's latest offering, the Home Safety Kit, which exemplifies the company's dedication to ensuring safety in residential spaces. Under Priya Nazareth's guidance, Monsher

India Safety Equipments continues to set the standard for safety and security solutions, making strides towards safer and more secure environments for all.

Prospects for Priya Nazareth: Monsher India Safety Equipments Pvt. Ltd.

Collaborators for Monsher India Safety Equipments Pvt. Ltd.

- Companies specializing in the production of safety equipment, who may collaborate with Monsher to expand their product range.

- Institutions focused on providing training in fire safety and security, who may partner with Monsher to offer practical training programs.

- Firms involved in designing and planning building structures, who may collaborate with Monsher to incorporate advanced safety systems into their designs.

- Consulting companies specializing in safety and security, who may collaborate with Monsher to offer comprehensive consulting services.

- Companies offering innovative technological solutions related to safety and security, who may collaborate with Monsher to integrate their technologies.

Clients for Monsher India Safety Equipments Pvt. Ltd.

- Firms involved in designing and constructing buildings, who require top-tier fire and security solutions for their projects.

- Companies engaged in real estate development seeking comprehensive safety and security systems for their properties.

- Individuals or firms specializing in safety consulting, who may partner with Monsher for expertise in fire and security solutions.

- Government agencies and municipalities are government bodies responsible for public safety and infrastructure, which may require advanced fire and security systems for various projects.

- Construction companies seeking reliable and efficient fire protection and security solutions for their projects.

- Companies that manage and maintain commercial and residential properties, which may require ongoing fire and security services.

- Educational institutions focused on fire and safety training that may seek partnerships or collaborations with Monsher for training programs or equipment.

- Corporate enterprises, seeking comprehensive fire and security solutions, are interested in solutions for their office spaces and facilities.

- Hotels, resorts, and hospitality businesses in need of fire protection and security systems to ensure the safety of guests and staff.

- Retail establishments and shopping malls seeking advanced fire and security solutions to safeguard their premises and customers.

- Hospitals and healthcare centres requiring specialised fire protection and security measures to ensure patient and staff safety.

- Educational institutions seeking reliable fire protection systems to ensure the safety of students and faculty.

- Residential communities seeking comprehensive fire safety and security solutions for the protection of residents and property.

- Companies involved in the manufacturing of fire and security equipment that may collaborate with Monsher for product development or distribution.

Potential Investors for Monsher India Safety Equipments Pvt. Ltd.

- Venture capital firms with a focus on safety and security solutions, who may see potential in investing in Monsher's innovative offerings.

- Private equity firms specializing in the construction and safety sectors, who may be interested in supporting Monsher's growth and expansion.

- Individuals with a high net-worth who have a personal interest in safety and security, and who may see value in investing in Monsher.

- Impact investors who seek to make a positive social or environmental impact through their investments, and who may be drawn to Monsher's commitment to safety.

- Investors with a background in the safety and security industry, who may have a deep understanding of the market and see potential in Monsher's offerings.

Write to: priya@monsher.com

Swpna Kulkarnii

About Swpna Kulkarnii's Venture:
Abhillabh Enterprises

Abhillabh Enterprises, operating under the distinguished trademark of Green Connect, embodies a vision deeply rooted in the pursuit of renewable

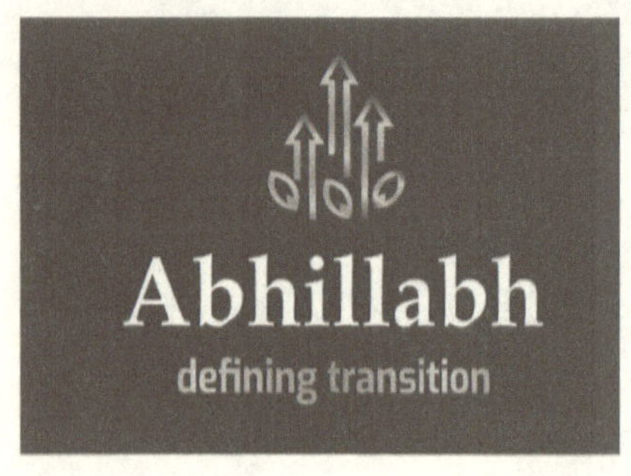

energy and sustainable practices. With a resolute commitment to green growth strategies, Abhillabh Enterprises aspires to contribute to economic and social well-being while fostering a sustainable environment.

Drawing from a robust foundation of energy management and conservation expertise, Abhillabh Enterprises boasts a team with over three decades of experience in renewable energy projects, thermal power plants, and steel plants. Their proficiency extends to maintenance, projects, engineering, and greenfield and brownfield projects. Additionally, the team possesses extensive knowledge in critical areas such as Total Productive Maintenance (TPM), SAP, ISO9000, Kaizen, Six Sigma, energy conservation, cost reduction, regulatory compliances, inventory analysis, maintenance planning, problem-solving techniques, and project planning.

> **Abhillabh Enterprises:** Pioneers of Renewable Energy and Green Growth

As a dynamic startup, Abhillabh Enterprises assumes the role of advisors and consultants in the renewable energy and waste-to-energy sectors. Their mission encompasses the promotion of various facets of green energy, including solar, wind, electric vehicles, energy storage, and hydrogen. Notably, they advocate for the conversion of AC transmission systems to DC transmission to curb energy loss and reduce power wastage.

Abhillabh Enterprises also champions LED lighting for its energy efficiency, cost-effectiveness, and sustainability benefits. Moreover, they actively promote electric vehicles, fostering a consumer mindset aligned with environmental betterment and decarbonization.

The company's ethos is underpinned by six pillars: customer-centricity, structural clarity, dependability, the meaningfulness of work, and the impact of effort. Abhillabh Enterprises offers a comprehensive range of services in the renewable energy domain, spanning rooftop and ground-mounted solar installations, waste-to-energy solutions, third-party inspection services, green hydrogen production, environmental clearances, and quality initiatives. Their commitment to building strategic partnerships and embracing the latest technologies positions them as trailblazers in the renewable energy sector. Abhillabh Enterprises is poised to usher in a greener and more sustainable future through its consultancy and solutions, setting new standards of excellence in the industry.

About Swpna Kulkarnii

Celebrating 26 years of dedication and persistence, Swpna Kulkarnii is a multifaceted leader who wears many hats with grace. She serves as the President of Mumbai's WEDO chapter, empowering women entrepreneurs and earning recognition as the 1st Fempreneur Awardee and a recipient of the Women's Achiever Award. Swpna is the Managing Director of Abhillabh Private Limited and Abhillabh Aagro Private Limited, focusing on renewable energy and sustainability through her initiative, Ggreen Connect.

In addition to her entrepreneurial prowess, Swpna is a holistic healer and the Founder of ASA Healing, a centre dedicated to transforming lives through inner self-discovery. With over a decade of experience as a Reiki Practitioner, she brings positivity and unique perspectives to her clients. Swpna is also delving into occult sciences, including numerology, tarot reading, playing card reading, and more, aiming to touch the lives of at least 10,000 individuals and help them discover their life purpose.

Swpna's journey as a customer-centric strategic leader is marked by a commitment to building strong partnerships and finding solutions that cater to customer needs. Her vision extends to contributing significantly to the growth of green energy, encompassing solar, wind, electric vehicle, energy storage, and hydrogen. Swpna Kulkarni's inspiring journey as an entrepreneur, healer, and advocate for positive change reflects her unwavering determination and a holistic approach to life and business.

Prospects for Swpna Kulkarnii: Abhillabh Enterprises

Collaborators for Abhillabh Enterprises

- Renewable energy experts enhance project execution and deepen understanding of the sector.

- Technology suppliers from abroad introduce cutting-edge innovations to India's renewable energy landscape, shaping the industry with their advancements.

- Government and regulatory bodies play a pivotal role as they facilitate seamless project approvals and ensure compliance, providing access to incentives in the renewable energy sector.

- Foster innovation and research in energy management and conservation within academic and research institutions.

- Business schools cultivate talent and nurture future leaders in the renewable energy domain.

Clients for Abhillabh Enterprises

- Industrial units keen on optimizing energy consumption and embracing sustainable practices.

- Hospitals and healthcare facilities looking to implement eco-friendly energy solutions, aligning with their commitment to well-being.

- Government agencies seeking energy-efficient solutions and compliance with environmental regulations.

- Real estate developers looking to incorporate green building practices and energy-efficient solutions.

- Private enterprises and corporations aspiring to transition to renewable energy sources.

Potential Investors for Abhillabh Enterprises

- Renewable energy investors engaging in green energy projects aligned with the future of sustainable power generation.

- Impact investors looking to support businesses with strong environmental and societal impact.

- Venture capital firms nurturing emerging players in the renewable energy arena.

- Private equity investors interested in sustainable energy ventures for potential investments and partnerships.

Write to: swpnakulkarnii@gmail.com

Dr. Revathi Rangaswamy

About Dr. Revathi Rangaswamy's Venture:
Bio 5 Irā Labs

Bio 5 Irā Labs, under the umbrella of Naadi Diagnostics, a promising newcomer in the healthcare & diagnostic arena, is poised to redefine industry standards by offering a comprehensive array of end-to-end diagnostic solutions. Comprising diagnostic labs, pharmacies, family clinics, wellness centres, and rural healthcare services for Tier 2 & Tier 3 towns. Bio 5 Irā Labs envisions a holistic healthcare ecosystem that sets it on a trajectory for success.

At the forefront of this endeavour is Bio 5 Irā Labs, a dedicated division committed to providing affordable and dependable pathology diagnostic services. Despite its relative newness, Bio 5 Irā Labs has garnered attention for its unwavering commitment to both illness and wellness sectors, aligning closely with the age-old wisdom "Prevention is better than cure."

Bio 5 Irā Labs: Elevating Healthcare Excellence

Bio 5 Irā Labs offers a wide spectrum of diagnostic tests from routine tests like CBC, blood sugars, LFTs to specialised testing like hormone profiling, cardiac markers, cancer markers to super specialised testing, including precision medicine, allergy testing, genetic analysis and chromosomal assessments, all rooted in a commitment to credibility and trustworthiness.

A standout offering from Bio 5 Irā Labs is its "Therapeutic Drug Monitoring TDS" testing division, a pioneering solution aimed at optimizing medication dosages for individuals prescribed common drugs. This reflects Bio 5 Irā Labs' dedication to precision medicine and personalised patient care.

Venturing into the wellness sector, Bio 5 Irā Labs responds to the evolving health consciousness of individuals aged 20 to 40. It presents a range of compact wellness packages meticulously tailored to address specific needs, such as the "Active Women Panel" and "Men Vitality Panel." These packages underscore Bio 5 Irā Labs' commitment to proactive well-being strategies that empower individuals to lead healthier, more fulfilling lives. While Bio 5 Irā Labs is relatively new, it already stands as a brand to watch in the healthcare landscape. With unwavering commitment to quality, innovation, and accessibility, Bio 5 Irā Labs is poised to make a significant impact, setting new benchmarks for healthcare excellence.

About Dr. Revathi Rangaswamy

Dr. Revathi Rangaswamy, a visionary entrepreneur, is the driving force behind Bio 5 Irā Labs. With a passion for healthcare and an entrepreneurial spirit, she embarked on a journey to transform the healthcare landscape.

Her motivation stems from the desire to create a brand that offers holistic healthcare solutions to the masses. Dr. Revathi's entrepreneurial journey is a testament to her commitment to bridging the gap between diagnostics, wellness, and accessibility.

As a healthcare professional herself, Dr. Revathi brings deep medical expertise to Bio 5 Irā Labs. Her unique perspective combines medical knowledge with business acumen, ensuring that the company's offerings are not only credible but also aligned with the evolving healthcare needs.

Prospects for Dr. Revathi Rangaswamy: Bio 5 Irā Labs

The main motto of Dr. Revathi Rangaswamy is to enable 100 aspiring women entrepreneurs to begin their journey of entrepreneurship through Bio 5 Irā Labs. The brand caters to the general public who prioritise excellence in healthcare. Individuals seeking accurate and reliable diagnostic services that focus on both illness and wellness can rely on Bio 5 Irā Labs for their healthcare needs.

Doctors, who value precision and quality in diagnostics choose Bio 5 Irā Labs for their practice. Corporate entities and HR departments seeking pre-employment checkups and employee health checks find comprehensive solutions here.

The company's emphasis on preventive healthcare resonates with those who understand the value of early detection and well-being. Ultimately, Bio 5 Irā Labs caters to clients who prioritise their health and seek trusted, credible, and accessible healthcare solutions.

Collaborators for Bio 5 Irā Labs

- Medical institutions providing the foundation for clinical excellence.

- Pharmaceutical giants partnering in pioneering research and developing innovative diagnostic approaches.

- Wellness centres becoming integral allies in promoting holistic well-being.

- Research institutions driving forward-looking advancements in diagnostics and healthcare solutions.

Clients for Bio 5 Irā Labs

- General public prioritizing excellence in healthcare.

- Individuals seeking accurate and reliable diagnostic services for both illness and wellness.

- Doctors valuing precision and quality in diagnostics.

- Corporate entities and HR departments seeking pre-employment checkups and employee health checks.

Potential Investors for Bio 5 Irā Labs

- Visionary investors passionate about advancing healthcare.

- Investors keen on healthcare innovation, technology, social impact, or wellness enhancement.

- Individuals or entities looking to make a meaningful impact in the healthcare sector and align with Bio 5 Irā Lab's mission of redefining healthcare excellence.

Write to: revathi2dr@yahoo.co.uk

Hema Raju

About Hema Raju's Venture: The Infinite Brain

The Infinite Brain stands as a beacon of transformation, a manifestation and coaching company that delves into the realms of personal coaching and manifestation meditation. With a profound commitment to unlocking human potential and fostering holistic well-being, Infinite Brain's offerings are designed to empower individuals on their journey to self-realization.

At the heart of the Infinite Brain's philosophy lies the art of manifestation—a practice that transcends the ordinary and taps into the extraordinary potential of the human mind. Through personal coaching, individuals are guided on a personalised journey of self-discovery, helping them navigate life's challenges, define their goals, and unlock their innate abilities.

> **The Infinite Brain:**
> Manifesting Dreams;
> Embracing a Limitless
> Future

One of the Infinite Brain's notable initiatives is the "Manifestation Gurukool." This transformative program serves as a testament to the company's dedication to training the brain to manifest and enabling people to realise their full potential. The Gurukool is a sanctuary of knowledge and wisdom, a space where the power of the brain and the art of manifestation are harnessed to facilitate holistic growth and self-fulfillment.

The Infinite Brain's vision extends beyond mere coaching. It is a conduit for individuals to harness the innate power of their minds, align with their true purpose, and manifest their dreams. Through the tools of personal coaching and manifestation meditation, the

Infinite Brain embarks on a mission to empower individuals to lead lives of abundance, purpose, and self-realization.

About Hema Raju

Hema Raju, a visionary entrepreneur at the age of 35, stands as a remarkable example of someone who seamlessly combines business acumen with a profound commitment to holistic well-being. Fluent in Tamil, Telugu, Hindi, and English, her linguistic versatility mirrors her ability to connect with a diverse audience.

Hema's entrepreneurial journey includes two notable ventures: "The Infinite Brain," where she serves as a manifestation mentor, and "PreciseGoal.com," a platform dedicated to mutual fund advisory. Her dedication to helping individuals manifest their aspirations and achieve financial security has earned her accolades, including the "Visionary Women Award" in 2023 from Max Life Insurance and the "International Peace Award" in 2020, recognised by the Lincoln Book of Records. These honors underscore her contributions to promoting peace, well-being, and financial literacy.

In the realm of education, Hema boasts an impressive array of qualifications. She holds a Master's degree in Business Administration and Finance, demonstrating her financial expertise, along with a Master's degree in Psychology. Her credentials further include an Advanced Diploma in School and Family Counseling, certification as a Motivational Interviewing Practitioner, NLP Master Life Coach, Reiki Healer, Silva Ultra Mind Level 4 graduate, and Emotional Freedom Tapping Practitioner. Hema's skills span subconscious mind programming, the Law of Attraction, the Law of Assumption, and cognitive behavioral therapy, all of which empower individuals to unlock their full potential and transform their lives.

In essence, Hema embodies a holistic well-being advocate and educator, where her fusion of business prowess and psychological insight empowers individuals to manifest their dreams, attain financial stability, and embrace lives of well-being and fulfillment.

Prospects for Hema Raju: The Infinite Brain

Collaborators for The Infinite Brain

- Business schools and communities interested in integrating spirituality into entrepreneurship.

- Alternative therapists and holistic practitioners seeking to co-create comprehensive well-being programs.

- Individuals and organisations looking to embark on journeys of personal and spiritual growth.

- Ideal partner for combining business acumen with spiritual wisdom for a conscious approach to life and entrepreneurship.

Clients for The Infinite Brain

- Entrepreneurs and business leaders seeking spiritual guidance in their ventures.

- Students, professionals, and individuals with special needs focusing on mental and emotional well-being.

- Athletes and sports enthusiasts for mental resilience and peak performance.

- Yoga studios and wellness centres for collaborative workshops.

- Seekers of spiritual growth and self-realization for insights into consciousness and inner transformation.

- Corporates aiming to enhance employee well-being and productivity through mindfulness programs.

- Versatile skill set and unwavering commitment to holistic wellness makes Hema a valuable resource for personal and spiritual growth seekers.

Potential Investors for The Infinite Brain

- Investors with a specific interest in this domain can explore opportunities with The Infinite Brain.

- The company specialises in personal coaching, manifestation meditation, and holistic well-being rooted in ancient Indian wisdom.

- Investors can tap into the global demand for alternative and spiritual wellness solutions through investments in The Infinite Brain's transformative initiatives.

Write to: manifestwithhema@infinitebrainacademy.com

Rashmi Coprum

About Rashmi Coprum's Venture: Jewellery Experience Academy

Jewellery Experience Academy is a testament to the dedication, expertise, and passion of its founder, who boasts over 15 years of experience in the industry. What began as a hobby in Jewellery Design in Bengaluru blossomed into a full-fledged vocation, leading to the pursuit of a diploma from the renowned GIA in New York. This initial foundation was further fortified with comprehensive training in various metal fabrications, gemstones, and CAD from esteemed Jewellery Trade Schools in New York and Bangalore.

At the heart of Jewellery Experience lies a distinct design philosophy characterised by three key principles: 'Light Weight,' 'Low Cost,' and 'Looks Stunning.' Every piece in their collection is a testament to their commitment, meticulously crafted with care, love, and an unwavering passion for their craft. Their specialties encompass Travel Jewellery, artisanal pieces, and the revival and transformation of treasured Heirloom Jewellery, showcasing a keen ability to infuse new life into cherished pieces of the past.

> **Jewellery Experience Academy:** Nurturing Future Jewellery Designers and Entrepreneurs with Passion, Expertise, and a Commitment to Craftsmanship

The belief that jewellery should be experienced, not merely worn, has driven the establishment of their latest endeavour: Jewellery Experience Academy. This visionary initiative aims to impart the art and science of jewellery-making as a viable career option to aspiring designers, budding entrepreneurs, and inquisitive enthusiasts alike.

Jewellery Experience Academy is the brainchild of Copparam Jewellers, a distinguished entity in Bangalore's esteemed Jewellery Street since its inception in 1999. With a rich legacy in the industry, Copparam Jewellers serves as the parent company, providing a solid foundation of expertise and craftsmanship for Jewellery Experience.

At the core of Jewellery Experience's offerings lies a diverse range of bespoke creations, encompassing gold, diamond, colored gemstones, and silver jewellery. Their repertoire includes not only the crafting of unique and customised pieces but also the skillful revitalization of vintage jewellery into contemporary masterpieces. Additionally, they provide curated options for jewellery gifting, ensuring that each piece carries with it a profound sense of thoughtfulness and sentiment.

Jewellery Experience Academy, a jewel in their crown, was inaugurated in October 2022. As a dedicated learning centre, it specialises in imparting knowledge and skills in Manual Jewellery Design, as well as Computer Aided Designs and Manufacturing. With a curriculum that covers both Rhino and Matrix, two prominent CAD jewellery design platforms, the academy equips its students with the tools and expertise needed to thrive in the dynamic world of jewellery design and production.

In summary, Jewellery Experience Academy stands as a testament to the fusion of passion, expertise, and a profound commitment to the art of jewellery-making. From the creation of stunning, personalised pieces to the nurturing of future talent through their academy, they continue to leave an indelible mark on the world of jewellery design and craftsmanship.

About Rashmi Coprum

Rashmi Coprum is a seasoned entrepreneur and visionary with over 15 years of experience in the jewellery industry.

In 2022, Rashmi embarked on a new venture, founding the Jewellery Experience Academy, dedicated to nurturing the next generation of jewellery designers, entrepreneurs, and enthusiasts. Her commitment to education extends to her role as a trainer in both Manual and CAD jewellery design.

Rashmi's journey is marked by significant achievements, including founding the successful Gold & Silver Jewelry boutique in Bengaluru and serving as a Professor at Vogue Institute of Design. Her expertise in silver smithing and fabrication, Keumboo Art, and Precious Metal Clay Jewelry sets her apart as a versatile artist.

What drives Rashmi is her aspiration to provide a platform for budding designers, especially women, in an industry that often offers limited opportunities. Her dedication to elevating the standards of jewellery design and production is evident in her transformative work, where vintage pieces find new life in contemporary wear. Rashmi Coprum's entrepreneurial spirit and commitment to mentorship are not just about crafting jewellery, but about empowering individuals to unleash their creative potential in this intricate art form.

Prospects for Rashmi Coprum: Jewellery Experience Academy

Collaborators for Jewellery Experience Academy

- Rashmi's extensive experience and knowledge in jewellery design could greatly benefit jewellery design schools and institutes, potentially leading to workshops, lectures, or joint educational programs.

- Rashmi's expertise in jewellery design and production could lead to collaborations in sourcing and utilizing gemstones effectively in jewellery pieces.

- Collaborations with experts in metalworking and fabrication could enhance workshops or training programs, providing students with a more comprehensive education in jewellery production.

- Rashmi's proficiency in computer-aided design (CAD) for jewellery could be valuable for software companies looking to refine or develop jewellery-specific CAD programs.

- Joint projects with fashion designers or fashion institutes could lead to innovative collaborations that combine jewellery and fashion in unique and marketable ways.

- Platforms like Etsy or similar online marketplaces could benefit from collaborations with Rashmi by featuring her designs or potentially hosting workshops or events.

- Collaboration with industry associations and participation in relevant events can provide valuable networking opportunities and exposure within the jewellery industry.

- Collaborating with jewellery manufacturers or studios could lead to internships, apprenticeships, or job placement opportunities for students trained by Rashmi.

- Joint efforts with associations representing traditional craftsmen could lead to skill-sharing and preservation of traditional jewellery-making techniques.

- Collaborations with programs supporting entrepreneurs could provide Rashmi with opportunities to mentor and guide aspiring jewellery designers and entrepreneurs.

- Rashmi's expertise could be valuable for online platforms offering courses in jewellery design, potentially leading to collaborations in course development or instructional content.

- Collaborations with experienced professionals can offer students additional perspectives and insights from those actively working in the jewellery industry.

Clients for Jewellery Experience Academy

- Individuals who are looking to enter the field of jewellery design and are seeking education and mentorship.

- Budding entrepreneurs in the jewellery industry are those interested in starting their own businesses and seeking guidance from an experienced industry professional.

- Students and enthusiasts of jewelry design transition seamlessly to people with a passion for jewelry-making and a desire to learn the art and science behind it.

- Experienced individuals looking to enhance their skills or transition into a new aspect of jewellery design and production.

- Women entrepreneurs, especially those interested in the jewellery industry, benefit from Rashmi Coprum's aim to provide opportunities and mentorship in this field.

- Individuals with existing skills in jewellery making who are looking to refine their techniques or explore new aspects of the craft.

- Students interested in CAD jewelry design, looking to gain expertise in computer-aided design for jewelry, particularly in platforms like Rhino and Matrix.

- Individuals interested in heirloom jewelry transformation include people who possess cherished heirloom pieces and are interested in having them transformed into contemporary jewellery.

- Potential customers for Rashmi Coprum's jewelry collection are individuals interested in lightweight, low-cost, and stunning jewelry, resonating with her design philosophy.

Potential Investors for Jewellery Experience Academy

- Investors with a focus on fashion and design may see value in supporting Rashmi's jewellery brand, especially if they believe in the potential for unique and trend-setting designs.

- Impact investors prioritise businesses with a positive social or environmental impact, considering investments in Rashmi's brand that align with their mission, particularly valuing her efforts to empower women in the jewelry industry.

- Established companies in the jewellery industry, such as manufacturers or retailers, may benefit from investing in Rashmi's brand as a way to diversify their product offerings or gain access to innovative design concepts.

Write to: Jewelleryexperienceacademy@gmail.com